Elizabeth

Learning to dress myself from the inside out

Elizabeth

Learning to dress myself from the inside out

For Liz –
The first to give me
valuable direction – I am
A memoir by *grateful –*
Mary Elizabeth Moloney *Lij Manny*

PUBLISHED BY

Heart
Whisperings

Elizabeth: Learning to dress myself from the inside out
by Mary Elizabeth Moloney

© 2012 Mary Elizabeth Moloney

Cover illustration and pen and ink drawings by Sheila Kennedy: www.smkennedyart.com

Book design by Nehmen-Kodner: www.n-kcreative.com

Printed in the United States of America
Published by: Heart Whisperings
http://heartwhisperings.wordpress.com

First Edition
ISBN: 978-0-9848097-0-7
Library of Congress Control Number: 2012900187

Dedicated to Ellen Sheire,
Jungian analyst and life teacher

The meaning of my existence is that life has addressed a question to me. Or conversely, I myself am a question which is addressed to the world, and I must communicate my answer, for otherwise I am dependent upon the world's answer.

—C. G. Jung
Memories, Dreams, Reflections

Contents

Foreword

White Fleecy Coat

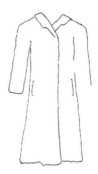

"**W**ell! Looks like your mother's still dressing you! So doll-like! Just like a cuddly polar bear in that coat!" So said my neighbor, his hooded bloodshot eyes scrutinizing my attire as I stepped into the mirrored elevator of the Lindell Terrace Condominium in St. Louis, Missouri, where I had lived since 1986. At his side stood his wife, silent rage tensing her sagging jowls.

I fidgeted with the clasp of the petit-point purse I carried, purchased by my maternal grandmother during one of her trips to Austria, then fixed my gaze upon my new black flats bought for Mother's annual Christmas party, to which I was headed.

How did my neighbor know? Did Mother's recent gift of my white coat, bought despite my objections, give me away? At sixty-seven years old, I was still her doll and hated it. Like the Nancy Ann Storybook Dolls she had given me as a child, my outfits told my story, because I had no story of my own. Only my bedroom mirror knew the shameful secret of my total enmeshment with Mother.

Elizabeth

The elevator inched its way to the garage, stopping on the fourth and third floors to pick up more neighbors.

Suddenly I felt pinned in a vortex. Around me spun significant dresses, sweaters, and blouses Mother had bought for me from the time I was a child. Here begins my story.

Part 1

How Mother Dressed Me,
1943–1967

1

First Holy Communion Dress, June 1943

It was the evening before my First Holy Communion. I was seven years old. Having long finished supper, I looked around the table: Mother, trim in her white piqué sundress and jacket and pearls, Dad in his tan business suit and tie, my older brother Tom still in his St. Louis Browns uniform, my younger, red-haired sister Martha in her sunsuit. My three-month-old brother John was upstairs with the nursemaid. Lost amid simultaneous conversations, I longed for Mother to ring for the cook, clear the table, and serve the apple pie she'd baked that afternoon. Then I could leave the table and climb the ash tree in the back yard and watch the sunset. There, alone, I was safe.

Suddenly, with a break in the chatter, Mother looked down the table at me, seated at Dad's left, and said, "Liz, let's have our dessert later. I want you to try on your new dress for tomorrow, to make sure it's all right." There'd already been three fittings at Miss Kopp's apartment in a walk-up in the Delmar Loop, each one because of growth spurts that piqued Mother's anger. It didn't take much for its explosion, and with it, Dad's wooden paddle from his Purdue University fraternity.

She rang for the cook, creating a diversion in the usual order of dinner. Feeling hot under everyone's gaze, I followed Mother up the carpeted stairs to my bedroom. The seams in her nylons were crooked, evidence of her haste in dressing for Dad's return from work and their cocktail hour before supper. Years before, her mother had recommended this afternoon ritual as a way to hold a husband's affections. It had worked for her and her stockbroker husband.

I slipped off my uniform school blouse and pleated navy skirt, then watched Mother shake out my white dress from the cellophane sleeve, untie the sash, and undo the buttons. While doing so, she spoke glowingly. "Years ago, Liz, I made my First Holy Communion at Visitation Academy—back in 1916." Her intense blue eyes sought mine, invited me into her world. For a split second, I warmed to her, as she smoothed a curl from her forehead. Her hair, styled in a pageboy, was brunette like mine. She continued, "I'll never forget my organdy dress and silk slip made by our seamstress; my lace veil with orange blossoms encircling the crown; my classmates' excitement over the dashing celebrant, Bishop Glennon; the candles we held while processing into the chapel; receiving Jesus for the first time; Sister Berchman's joy; then home with my jubilant family and the party in my honor." On and on Mother went, her euphoria inciting mine. Like her, I was soon to become another little bride of Christ. Fifteen years later I would become a real bride of Christ, a novice nun, during the clothing ceremony in Albany, New York, but more of that later.

Slowly, I raised my arms as Mother lifted the dress over my head, then thrust my hands into the sleeves. The dress had to fit, but it didn't. The sleeves squeezed my upper arms like sausage casings.

"No!" Mother said, her blue eyes steeling, her mouth hardening. "This is awful! Liz, I told you not to eat between meals! You can't make your First Communion without this dress! What will my parents say? And the others, coming for brunch tomorrow?" On and on she ranted. I pulled back from her. She yanked the dress over my head and tore out of the room, seeking Dad.

Alone in my new slip with rosettes stitched to the bodice, I sank to the floor, relieved Mother had not spanked me or yelled, "Get out of my sight with those black eyes, you thing, you! You disgust me!" as she usually did when cross.

Again, Dad relieved a testy situation by returning my dress to Miss Kopp's for alteration and picking it up an hour before we were due at Our Lady of Lourdes, a Norman Gothic-style church built in St. Louis County in 1919.

That morning I fidgeted on the kneeler among twenty-six classmates: the boys in navy jackets and white knickers, the girls in white dresses. Mine had a square neckline trimmed with Irish lace. The sleeves bit into my arms, as did gartered white stockings into my thighs. I felt queasy. Again, Dad looked through the lens of his movie camera as I approached the church doors at the end of the procession of my classmates. I was expected to smile. Instead I fumed, lowered my gaze to my new white prayerbook, my white tulle veil sloping over my stooped shoulders, and hurried inside. Ethereal strains from the organ in the choir loft created a festive mood for families already jammed in the pews.

Woozy from last night's fast, I folded my hands upon the pew and waited with my classmates for directions from Sister Mary Emily, our second-grade teacher, habited in black, a starched white wimple enclosing her thin face. Fans droned, circulating the hot air, as the organist played another interlude. Perspiration matted my braids, tied with white bows beneath a ribbed cap that held my veil and numbed my ears. Somewhere behind me knelt my parents, brother Tom, and my relatives: the Costigans with blue eyes, the Moloneys with brown eyes.

Bells jangled from the sacristy. Everyone stood to welcome the pastor, Monsignor Francis J. O'Connor, his white fiddleback chasuble tied upon his spindly frame; behind him shuffled two servers in black cassocks and starched white surplices. After bowing at the foot of the altar, the Monsignor rasped, "*In nomine Patri—et Filio et—Spiritu Sancto.*" The Mass was beginning. I opened my prayerbook as I was supposed to, but did not read. Instead, my gaze soared above the sanctuary to the gilt-framed canvas, conceived in the style of Titian: an angel staying the knife that Abraham held over his only son Isaac, who lay bound atop a sacrificial mound of wood. Its horror had mesmerized me ever since my parents began bringing me to this church.

After more Latin prayers, the parishioners tensed as the Monsignor nodded to the ushers to turn off the fans and lurched toward the pulpit. It was time for the Scripture reading and the sermon. His dour looks, his wagging fingers, always silenced me. I felt faint, still clutching my prayerbook. More kneeling and Latin prayers followed.

My classmates and I stood. I noted Sister Mary Emily's ethereal smile, signaling us to sing, "O Sacrament Most Holy," a hymn we'd practiced for weeks. My cottony mouth produced no sounds. The drama escalated toward receiving Jesus for the first time.

Again, Sister signaled us, this time, to file out of the pews and kneel before the communion rail. A great hush settled over the worshippers. Incense sweetened the air. I waited my turn.

Glancing sideways, I heard the Monsignor mumble something and saw shaky hands place the sacred Host on my classmates' tongues.

Then the server, one scuffed tennis shoe atop the other, paused in front of me and held the gold paten under my chin lest the Monsignor drop the sacred Host. I shut my eyes, leaned my head back, opened my mouth, then received Jesus from the Monsignor's gnarled fingers. My heart pounded as blinding Light opened me to shimmering fields, to silence imbued with sweetness, to bliss. Tears welled in my brown eyes. Never had I been so loved.

Later I became invisible during Mother's elegant brunch for my relatives—the women in straw hats with modesty veils, white gloves stashed in purses slung over their forearms; the men in shirtsleeves and ties loosened at their necks, their suit coats draped over chairs—guffawing, smoking, sipping Bloody Marys. They were a curious lot, jamming the lower floor of our spacious home.

At the turn of the twentieth century, these first-generation Irish Catholic families, the blue-eyed Costigans and the brown-eyed Moloneys, had lived across the street from each other on Raymond Avenue in North St. Louis. Mother's father, a tense, spindly man with sparse white hair, started work as a clerk with a brokerage firm, Whitaker and Company, and through shrewd investments worked his way up to a vice-presidency. My other grandfather, called "The Gov," was a transformer repairman with Laclede Gas Company. After learning how to make transformers at less cost, he founded his own company in 1892. As both families prospered, they found better neighborhoods, the Moloneys choosing Pershing Avenue in the Parkview area near Washington

University; the Costigans choosing a place on Lindell Boulevard, across from Forest Park, with a carriage house for stabling their horses. Mother enjoyed riding and the easy access from there to trails in Forest Park. When gathered for events such as my First Holy Communion, these families coated their tensions with Dewar's scotch, cigarettes, and Pat-and-Mike jokes.

Only aromas of scrambled eggs, sausage, and bacon from the kitchen grounded me. Always hungry, I looked forward to the sweet rolls Mother had ordered from Lake Forest Bakery and decorated mints from Bissinger's.

Finally it was time to open the white-ribboned gifts stacked upon the living-room coffee table and floor. Still awed by the blinding Light experience, I reached for a heavy package and pulled away the wrappings to discover a two-foot-tall statue of the Sacred Heart of Jesus. My maternal grandmother sitting in a wingback chair behind me reached over and hugged my shoulders and said, "Liz, I wanted you to have this on your special day. The women in our family have always drawn strength from this devotion." A single tear streaked her powdered cheek, and she added, "In time, you'll learn more about it."

Unexpectedly, my heart warmed as I cradled the heavy statue in my lap, oblivious to noisy relatives surrounding me. I was drawn toward another world, somehow related to the blinding Light experience earlier that morning. Even the strawberry stains on my ill-fitting First Holy Communion dress did not matter. Later I enshrined the Sacred Heart statue on the bookcase in my bedroom. Within its aura I thrived.

2

Gibson Girl Blouse and Plaid Skirt, January 1947

Unusually tall for my twelve years and still hefty, I pitched my shoulders to hide budding breasts that were nudging me into adolescence. I feared they would become like Mother's, mashed into the all-in-one foundation garment she had worn since she was a teenager, at her mother's behest. Her peers at Visitation Academy had done so as well, eager to display their svelte bodies under gossamer tea gowns in each other's parlors. Looking elegant comprised their initiation into womanhood; its sole purpose was to attract successful Catholic mates and start families, raise more Catholics. There was no reason to seek a deeper meaning in their femininity.

With that mindset, Mother sought to raise me. Before family outings to Busch's Grove, the Missouri Athletic Club, Cardinals baseball games at Sportsmen's Park, or Sunday Mass at the parish church, she checked my outfit, then scolded, "Liz! Stand straight! Throw your shoulders back! If you don't, you'll develop scoliosis of the spine! Then you won't be able to breathe." Schooled in her mother's perfectionism, she abhorred any deviation from the norm.

Months passed with more scoldings.

Exasperated by my noncompliance, Mother finally had me outfitted for a shoulder brace that cut into my armpits; it became synonymous with her rage when I chose not to wear it or not perform the back exercises the physical therapist had recommended. We never spoke about other bodily changes; they just happened.

But I did change grade schools. It happened quickly. I was alone, on Wydown Boulevard, walking home from Our Lady of Lourdes. September winds flitted maple leaves along the sidewalk. Across from me, a green sedan slowed to a stop, and a balding, clean-shaven man climbed out. He looked upset. One coat sleeve flapped behind him. Something bulged in the front of his buttoned raincoat. He called, "Hello! You there! I need help for my sick piggy! Do you know where I can find a doctor?" I froze. His urgent need conflicted with Mother's counsel never to speak to strangers, although I never knew why.

In halting tones, I directed him to Forest Park and the St. Louis Zoo several miles east of us. "Thanks," he said, his crooked smile revealing stained teeth. Then he stepped back and added, "Well, can you beat that? There's been a change. I can feel it." He peered down the front of his overcoat, patted the bulge with his other hand. "I think my piggy has to vomit." Then he shoved something pink through the opening of his overcoat, and it spewed a wide arc of yellow fluid, spraying the nearby bushes. Satisfied, he drove off.

"You did what?" Mother yelled, wiping her hands on her housedress. "You never do what I tell you to do! Get away from me with those black eyes!" Stung again, I sought refuge with the Sacred Heart statue in my bedroom. After lighting the votive candle, I sank to the floor and hid out in the shadows.

With no explanation, Mother transferred me to Villa Duchesne, a twelve-grade academy in West St. Louis County that offered door-to-door transportation. The first morning I climbed onto Arthur's bus, I felt conspicuous in my new blue uniform jumper and jewel-neck blouse that gave me an even fuller figure. My classmates, svelte in theirs, had their own friends. Fat and lonely and invisible, my resentments festered. The Mothers of the Society of the Sacred Heart who taught in the school seemed oblivious to my distress.

After months of painful isolation emerged a solution: to wear more grownup clothes to the few birthday parties I was invited to, clothes like those in the glossy photos featured in the magazine *Seventeen*. In a weak moment, Mother let me shop alone in the Teen department at the Famous-Barr department store, where my classmates bought their trendy outfits. Until that afternoon, Mother had selected my dresses from the Chubette Department in the same store.

Alone in the dressing room, the stool in the corner, Mother's accustomed place, empty, I slipped the Gibson Girl blouse from the hanger. It must fit. So far so, so good. I threaded my arms through the long sleeves, buttoned the back, and admired the stitched yoke. Size 14 worked. Next the red wool plaid circle skirt with green fringe on the hem, just as my classmates wore. Sucking in my gut, I fastened the side buttons and smiled at the beginnings of my waistline.

Later, Mother raised her eyebrows when she saw the outfit I had charged to her account, but because it did not adversely affect the budget Dad allotted her, she let me keep it.

No more was said about the matter, but in fantasy, I often wore my Gibson Girl blouse and circle skirt, pumped up by others' adulation, especially Aunt Jane's. A redhead with shoulder-length hair, she was my mother's youngest sister. Recently during an overnight visit at my newly-widowed grandmother's house, I had watched her and her physician fiancé kiss in the front hall after their date. Such a long and hungry kiss I had never seen before. My parents showed no such passion, only pecks on cheeks as they came and went. The next morning, as we sat around the breakfast-room table, my aunt smiled warmly at me as I toyed with steaming oatmeal around the edges of the bowl. I had felt so grown up.

The following January, Aunt Jane and her sweetheart would marry in the St. Louis Cathedral. It was the perfect occasion to wear my grown-up outfit. I couldn't wait.

On the morning of the wedding, Mother's brunette hair was still in curlers, smoke rings wreathing her face, as she called after me from the breakfast room, "Liz, you're to wear the outfit Miss Kopp made for you last month. It's laid out on your bed. Your sister will wear hers. Now hurry up. We've not much time."

I cringed at the sharp edge in her voice and trudged upstairs to my bedroom. Flopping on my bed, I silently screamed to the mirror above the dresser. Such a face! Those black eyes again! Next to me lay the white blouse smocked in burgundy and the matching knife-pleated skirt that drew attention to my thick hips. Martha's outfit was like mine but in Kelly green. In a split second, however, I had a way around this impasse.

After brushing my thick hair, now permanented like Mother's every three months at Marie's Salon, I shoved the designated outfit back into my closet, put on the Gibson Girl blouse and circle skirt, preened in the mirror, then went downstairs for my long coat. Seated in the back seat of our Oldsmobile parked in the driveway, my knees shivering with the cold, I studied my white socks and black flats and waited for the others. My brother Tom gave me a sour look and my sister Martha a surly one, as they crammed in next to me. Then we were off to the wedding, a society wedding like my parents' in 1932.

With Mother in the lead, we paraded to our designated pew in the St. Louis Cathedral. It resembled a spring garden with white roses flanking the marble altar beneath a wrought-iron balustrade soaring into a central dome resplendent with mosaics. The great organ spun gossemer webs upon the worshippers below. Excitement mounted as my aunt's bridesmaids began their procession down the main aisle. Next came my aunt, an ecstatic bride enveloped in mounds of satin and lace, on the arm of her brother Ed. Everyone stood. Her groom, a white rose in the lapel of his morning suit, grinned, awaiting her at the sanctuary gates.

I could barely contain myself. Their kiss that night, and perhaps others, had somehow led to this morning's radiance. Still caught up in the drama, I was unaware of my coat parting when I knelt down as the celebrant began the prayers at the foot of the altar. Suddenly I shivered under Mother's icy gaze. She knew. "Just look at you!" she spat. "You never do anything I say! You exasperate me! If there was time, we'd go home so you could change." Dad looked on, his brown eyes meeting mine. For once, he understood, but could do nothing.

Helpless under her thumb, I cowered. I had no words, never did. Her abuse cut me to the quick. I was becoming "the thing" she so hated.

Elizabeth

Mother's tongue-lashing continued in the cloakroom at Glen Echo Country Club, the elegant setting for the reception. As she removed her Persian lamb coat and handed it to the uniformed attendant, she muttered, "Such a tacky outfit! Stay away from me. You embarrass me!" Grabbing her clutch purse, she took Dad's arm and circulated among the guests; among them, her ill humor soon vanished. I sulked and sought the buffet table in the dining room and the distraction of food.

Stuffed with wedding cake, my plaid skirt pinching my waist, I perched on a striped chair next to the balcony overlooking the chatting wedding guests, their drinks and cigarettes in gloved hands. Even Mother looked happy in her black wool dress with its lace-trimmed collar and cuffs studded with rhinestones. Dad stood tall at her side, listening. He always seemed to do that. With my finger, I traced the plaids in my circle skirt, sorely aware that Aunt Jane had not noticed me, much less smiled as she had on other occasions. She was lost in the arms of her new husband, twirling on the dance floor, surrounded by well-wishers.

When we returned home, I knew there would be more from Mother, and there was. Never again was I to shop without her supervision. Never again would I embarrass her with outfits I liked. The next week, she bundled up the Gibson Girl blouse and wool plaid circle skirt for the Goodwill pickup. Thereafter, we shopped in the Chubette Department at Famous-Barr. As my waistline expanded, my posture worsened.

3

Red Strapless Tea Gown, February 1951

More years passed. Despite my height of five feet, seven inches, despite my beginner's bra, I felt like a block of rough-hewn wood, awkward, invisible. Nevertheless, it was time for Mother to present me to her friends and my classmates at a formal tea in our house. Her mother had also introduced her to the society of her friends and had told stories laced with high drama and of fastidious preparations. For this occasion, I needed a gown, pumps dyed to match. Instead of shopping in the Chubette Department, Mother and I rode the bus to Montaldo's, a fashionable store in the Central West End. Low-hanging clouds spit chilly rains as we pulled open the glass doors and stepped inside this pricey world of choice fabrics and colors. Soothing Muzak massaged our tension as we headed toward the second floor and sought a saleslady. Other well-heeled customers, fixated upon some inner need, meandered around counters displaying handbags, accessories.

Elizabeth

After settling in our spacious fitting room, Mother unbuttoned her tweed coat, tucked her scarf in one of the sleeves, and tossed it upon the velour loveseat in the corner. No stool here. Above us, recessed lights were trained upon a dais surrounded by mirrored walls. Our saleslady had already hung frothy gowns, most of them strapless, on brass knobs encircling us. From them, Mother would make her selection. It would be a long morning.

Reluctantly, I began removing my clothes. Mother scrutinized my body. The mirrors were also looking at my ever-changing girth. Trapped within their truth, I numbed out.

"You'll need a strapless bra," the saleslady said, passing one through the parted curtain. "This should fit. Perhaps this waist-cincher to accentuate your figure," she added.

Funny looking things, I thought, but I knew not to object. Standing in my panties and half-slip, I hooked the garments in place. The effect was startling, despite my difficulty breathing.

"Are you decent?" the saleslady asked, then parted the curtains and headed toward the gowns, her flushed cheeks anticipating a handsome sale. "Let's see which of these will work best for you. Your mother wants you to look special."

"We can manage from here," Mother said, smoothing a stray curl from her tense forehead, then folding her arms. "I'll call if I need your help."

"But, Mother, most of these gowns are strapless," I said in a wispy tone. "We're not supposed to wear them. Mother Scott said we'd get in trouble if we did." For months during Politeness classes, the Mistress General of Villa Duchesne, prim in her long black habit and starched cap and veil, had urged us to abide by the protocols set by the "Supply the Demand for the Supply." This was a movement established by the heads of local Catholic all-girl high schools to discourage shop owners from carrying strapless gowns, deemed immodest. When shopping for tea or graduation gowns, we were to request ones with sleeves.

"I'm aware of that," Mother said, "but each of these gowns comes with a tulle stole that can be tucked into the bodice to cover your shoulders. You'll be all right. Now let's try on this pink one."

I worked through mounds of tulle and lace, heady with fresh smells, then pulled the bodice to my waist as Mother zipped up the back.

"Now stand on the dais, and throw your shoulders back, so I can see," Mother said, somehow energized by this challenge.

I did so, barely breathing, awaiting the decision. A pinkish blur looked back at me in the mirror.

"No, that won't do. Makes you look sallow. We can't have that. Here's a white one. Let's try that."

The white one was too skimpy. Others were too big, too long, too tight. I was beyond weary at this point, but Mother continued her pursuit of the perfect gown. It turned out to be a fire-engine-red tulle strapless gown with tracings of gold filigree across the bodice.

Even I was surprised standing on the dais, my brown eyes agog. Who was this young woman smiling at me in the mirror everywhere I turned? Could this be me?

Mother was pleased as well. "Red is your color, Liz," she said, helping me out of the gown, then checking the sales tag. "It's more than I planned to spend, but I want you to look elegant for your presentation."

It was three o'clock, time for the tea party in our oak-paneled dining room ablaze with flaming candles set in candelabra on the buffet and window wells. Two years before, we had moved into a mottled-yellow brick Tudor Revival home with a blue-grey slate roof, designed by the distinguished architectural firm Raymond Maritz and Ridgely Young. Each room was a showcase of complementary textures and tones. Here, Mother was following her mother's penchant for sumptuousness.

The tulle stole of my new gown scratched my shoulders, as I settled my skirts in front of Mother's sterling silver coffee urn banked by her china cups and saucers. An epergne of red roses, white carnations and chrysanthemums sat upon a handmade lace cloth from Brussels. China platters held one-of-a-kind cheese puffs, chestnuts wrapped in bacon, finger sandwiches, pastries, and chocolates. A punch bowl filled with orange sherbet and ginger ale stood on the buffet. I was, indeed, "pretty at the table," as my maternal grandmother had predicted at my birth, but I was not "pretty" on the inside.

Suddenly, something jarred me from this fairytale world in which I was supposed to be the princess. It was Dad, stealing a look at me on his way to his office at Moloney Electric Company. I felt naked, despite the strapless bra mashing my breasts. My hands, enfolded in my skirts, shook hard.

Then Mother's voice, as from a distant realm, pierced this malaise. "Liz, don't forget to hold yourself straight. Throw those shoulders back!" she said, straightening crystal cups around the punch bowl and relighting a candle that had gone out. Her white lace gown set off her matronly figure; a slipper orchid was pinned to her shoulder. And always her signature fragrance, *L'Air du Temps.*

Romantic strains played on the Capehart in the living room. Exquisite aromas from the kitchen mingled with the forced heat in our home. Aproned servers stood in the dining room and front hall, waiting to greet and serve our guests.

All was ready, but where were they? Would my Villa Duchesne classmates come? Only one had sent a flower arrangement. I'd expected more, having sent gifts to their coming-out parties, then enduring awkward moments around their tea tables until it was appropriate to leave. They still excluded me from their inner circles, viewed me as dumb. At the time, I was unaware of the learning disorder that was playing havoc with my concentration.

Further compounding my distress were stories of Mother's successes at tea parties and country club dances she had attended as a teenager; stories her mother shared during my overnights in her apartment in The Netherby, east of what had been her elegant house on Lindell Boulevard. She had moved there after her husband's death in 1943.

"Come, Liz," Grandmother had said, snapping open the gold watch hanging around her neck on her full bosom, "Let's go to my bedroom. From there we can watch the Cotillion. It's already begun." Excitement spirited her steps across the Oriental rugs. Another story was coming. After pulling armchairs next to the opened window, we gazed into the evening, softened by May breezes. Next door was The St. Louis Women's Club, an elegant residence established in the early 1900s to house and entertain dignitaries attending the St. Louis World's Fair. On the top floor was a ballroom, where musicians played for young teens wearing formal attire and woodenly moving upon the dance floor.

Grandmother fingered her pearls. She said, "Liz, your mother was such a beauty, such a joy to dress, despite the occasional annoyances with dressmakers. I remember that time in Paris. I'd insisted she have a Paris frock—a pink lacy number by an eminent designer. Not knowing when her next soiree would occur, I had to be ready. Rarely did she wear the same gown—that just wouldn't do," she added, her blue eyes dreaming. "Besides, her classmates at Visitation would have gossiped."

Suddenly next door, the music paused and couples parted and headed toward tables laden with bouquets and refreshments. A few girls giggled to friends behind gloved hands. Others checked their watches. Grandmother was all eyes. Her story continued. "Unlike those girls, your mother was always gracious around boys. They flocked to be her escort—and when we announced her engagement to your father, many asked which Tom was the lucky man."

Like Mother that afternoon of the tea, I was dressed to the nines, but had no stories of conquests to share with my Villa Duchesne classmates.

The doorbell rang. From the entrance hall came the voices of Kit and her twin sister Marie. They'd sent the red roses displayed on the baby grand piano in the living room.

"Liz!" Kit exclaimed in a throaty voice, stepping into our dining room, stashing her kid gloves inside her beaded purse. "How lovely everything is! A privilege to be here!"

It was beginning. I had to perform—make conversation, pour coffee from the urn. The tulle bodice irritated my bare arms. Stress worked its way down my neck. "Hi, Kit!" I somehow managed. "Would you like some coffee?"

"Sure would. It's bitter cold out. Nearly froze driving over here. My heater's on the blink," she said, the gold charms on her bracelet jangling. "Marie would like some, too," she added. Both wore ruby wool dresses with long sleeves buttoned at their wrists.

Again, the doorbell rang. This time it was Harriet and Ann, both wearing black taffeta circle skirts enhanced by crinolines, jeweled blouses, and three-inch heels. In no time, they were sipping punch and nibbling butter cookies while making small talk with Mother, now nursing her glass of wine. I gripped my hands and waited.

More minutes passed. The dining room still appeared festive, but largely empty.

The doorbell, again. It was Aunt Jane and some of Mother's friends from Visitation Academy and Maryville College, come to relive the elegant teas of their teenage years. A flurry of hugs and commendations of my gown ensued, then reminiscences of their shining moments. Again I was alone. Mother stood tall in her lace pumps, puffed up by their adulations of her daughter, of her exquisite table. She had become more than adept as a hostess, now having years of parties behind her. A far cry from the time of her marriage, when she'd only known how to boil an egg, make fudge, and bake lemon meringue pie.

Suddenly Aunt Jane pulled away from her listeners, wanting more coffee. She was plumper now for having had two children. Although she was weary, her bright smile warmed me, and my hand did not shake as much handing her the creamer. "It's been a while since I've seen you, Liz," she said, placing the spoon on her saucer. "You're becoming quite a lady. Your mother must be so pleased." I pulled up in my arm chair, the tulle stole slipping off my ivory shoulders to my elbows. I had been seen.

However, the continuing emptiness of this festive dining room numbed me. I felt soulless, like one of my Nancy Ann Storybook dolls with painted smiles—only mine ached. Mother, too, was upset, furtively checking her diamond wristwatch while chatting with her friends. She had prepared for fifty guests.

A half hour later, the romantic tunes on the Capehart having played out, our home emptied after thanks and goodbyes. Within chilling silence, aproned servers began clearing the table and buffet and putting away the food.

Mother gave me a dour look as she blew out the candles and said, "Well, it's over—all this effort, and for what? I told you repeatedly to get those invitations in the mail sooner than you did. No wonder so few came."

Her truth stung. To no one had I disclosed my hope that the tea party would fail. Rather than expose myself to snickers of my classmates, I chose to sabotage Mother's party. And it worked, despite backfiring upon me.

I retreated to my bedroom and pulled off the gown that had become a nightmare of frothy elegance. Dressing up like this was too costly.

Mother and I never spoke of that afternoon, its February chill congealing my spirit. But Aunt Jane had glimpsed the woman I would become. That I would remember.

My red strapless gown, bagged and hung in the hall closet among Mother's cocktail dresses, gathered dust. A year passed before I wore it again, to Villa's Junior-Senior dance at the Congress Hotel, another awkward occasion.

In the interim, I continued finding solace in my devotions to the Sacred Heart statue in my bedroom. He was always available.

4

Black Velvet Sheath,
December 1956

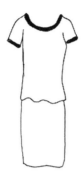

My hand shook applying eyeliner around my brown eyes, stinging from sleepless nights. Soon I would see Joe Gummersbach, newly discharged from the Army, my date for a college friend's engagement party. Before the end of the evening, Joe would learn that my future plans did not include him. Why I chose this occasion to break his heart again indicated my lack of compassion. It was all about me.

Four years before, Mother had arranged my first date with Joe for the Villa Duchesne graduation dance. The college-aged son of one of her bridge partners, he was tall, barrel-chested, with searching amber eyes and peppery speech. His white tux complemented his tanned face. Despite his ineptness on the dance floor, I thrilled at being in his arms, occasionally sniffed his double gardenia corsage on my wrist. When the orchestra began playing "Good Night, Sweetheart," the last dance, Joe's gaze set me afire. Picking up the skirts of my strapless white gown with a sequined bodice, I followed him to the dance floor, felt his heaving chest upon mine.

Over the summer, we enjoyed Cokes and movie dates, his Holy Cross ring mashing my fingers in darkened theaters. Soft kisses beneath the overhead fixture at my back door simultaneously warmed and terrified me. Thanksgiving break, my college roommate and I took the train to Manhattan and checked into the Biltmore Hotel, thronged with other students meeting friends under the famous clock in the lobby. There, I met Joe for another movie date, a rendezvous previously arranged through letters from his Worcester, Massachusetts, campus. Never had I been so loved. I felt tingly all over. However, a line from "The Song from Moulin Rouge" dampened my mounting passion: "It's a sad thing to realize/that you've a heart that never melts." New Year's and a night of French kissing in his heated car finally broke the spell. I bolted, convinced I was in mortal sin clearly enunciated by Jesuits during days of retreat at Villa Duchesne.

The story went like this: A Catholic teenage couple rented a canoe and paddled to the middle of the lake in Forest Park. Before long, they began fondling each other. Their kisses became more inflammatory, tongues sucking, pulling. That was called French kissing, "a mortal sin absolved only within the sacrament of penance," the Jesuit had said in solemn tones. Suddenly the couple's gyrations upset the canoe and both drowned, and their fate was hellfire for all eternity.

Then, while vacationing with my family in La Jolla, California, we ran into Joe and his priest brother after Sunday Mass. That night they joined us for supper at the Del Charro Restaurant. It had been three years since that night in Joe's car. Beneath small talk over our seafood dishes, old passions stirred anew. His manliness silenced me. His probing eyes again sought entrance into my world. I shivered. No mention of my having broken his heart.

Afterwards in the shadowy parking lot, he reached for my hand and blurted, "Liz, I had hoped to see you again. What were the chances of it happening like this?" Ocean breezes mussed his short brown hair. From somewhere, a bird's trill split the night.

I nodded, still speechless, again feeling the pressure of his Holy Cross ring, of my waist cincher beneath my turquoise dress.

Joe moved closer, his eyes feverish, and said, "I hope we can get together when I get out of the Army—later this year." His intelligence work at his station in Baltimore had only heightened his attractiveness.

Our letters resumed, and with them, my determination to lose the weight caused by devouring chocolates and buttered Wonder Bread. Joe was in love with me, and I was in love with him. This time I'd stand my ground and not flee. Not trusting anyone, I decided to work this out on my own.

The following October during my senior year at Maryville College, Mother's alma mater, I learned Mother had plans for me. "Liz," she said, noting my attractive silhouette as I walked into the family room, "soon you'll be twenty-one. It's time you owned some cocktail dresses, something more sophisticated than your black one." Immediately, I sensed her agenda—to outfit me for society and snare a husband as she had. "Let's go to Montaldo's and see what they have," she added, her blue eyes brightening. Again standing upon the dais in the mirrored fitting room, I felt awkward under her scrutiny trying on designer dresses, each more luxurious than the next. This time, price was not a consideration. Hours passed. Finally, the selection narrowed to two cocktail dresses: a black velvet sheath and a lime-colored lace dress that enhanced my shoulders. In them I looked stunning. I would have both.

Then in November, Mother Scott, who had become the Dean of Women at Maryville, had called me to her office for her usual talk to seniors before their twenty-first birthdays. Never had I spoken with her alone. I found her poring over a letter on her barrel-top desk beneath a single brass lamp that cast light-webs upon a twenty-foot ceiling. I knocked.

"Why, good evening, Liz. Come in and sit by me. I hear you'll soon be twenty-one, that your thesis on English ballads is coming along nicely," she said, her pursed lips slightly parted, her silky black veil sliding over the sides of her starched cap. Taken aback by her ingratiating invitation, I nodded, jammed my fists in the pockets of my charcoal skirt, and approached her, the Oriental rug swallowing my footfalls.

After inquiring about my family, she asked, "Have you thought what you'll do after graduation? I heard you've spent summers as a nurse's aide at St. Mary's Hospital." Again I nodded, hugged my arms through the sleeves of my blazer, then jiggled my penny loafers. "Might you go into the field of nursing? Certainly you could do a lot of good for patients." I shook my head, always having been relieved after my shift to peel off my perspiration-soaked uniform. Only a few rooms on the surgical floor I covered were air-conditioned. Behind Mother Scott, winds tossed specter branches against the tall windows in the lowering dark.

My discomfort mounted. Leaning toward me, her grey eyes alight behind rimless glasses, she continued, "I understand you received your Child of Mary medal while at Villa Duchesne. Quite a distinction at such a young age, usually bestowed upon older sodalists advanced in prayer."

I gripped the armrests, struck dumb. How did she know? Another had replaced her as Mistress General the year before my graduation.

She pressed her silver profession cross upon her chin, looked intently at me, and added, "Often I've seen you kneeling in the chapel, afternoons, when I'm there. Do you know your piety impresses your classmates? They've told me so." I reeled with this disclosure. She paused, her eyes misting, then asked, "My child, have you ever thought you might be blessed with a religious vocation, perhaps to the Society? You know our noviceship is in Albany, New York."

I blanched. How did she know I had been attracted to the convent during days of recollection at Villa Duchesne and later at Maryville, and how that attraction had quickly dissipated upon returning to my designer bedroom and the latest issue of *Seventeen*? The black habits of nuns always repulsed me; in warmer weather, they smelled.

"You look uncomfortable, Liz. Tell me what's on your mind. You know I'm only here to help you," Mother said, a faint smile parting her creased lips. Under her gaze, I felt like a specimen wiggling upon a pin in a botany lab.

Suddenly, tears flash-flooded me. I could not stop. She had sparked fire, long denied. "You and the others seem to know God," I blurted. "I've always wanted that but never knew how to go about it—even ached to belong to God like you all do, yes, even become a member of the Society. Your joy's so deep." I wiped my eyes with the sleeve of my blazer, then mumbled, "But I'm not sure."

"No matter for now, my child," she said, her veined hands toying with her sidebeads, breaking the awful stillness between us. "You've opened your heart to me this evening, and I will keep in confidence all that you shared. Let's ask God's guidance for your future."

"It's funny our conversation moved in this direction," I said, recovering my voice, fingering Joe's last letter in my pocket. "I'd planned to speak with you about my boyfriend. He'll be home from the Army next month." A curious smile flickered on the Dean's narrow lips, as her back stiffened. "It seems like he wants to get back together. I don't know about that either."

"Well, let's just see what happens," Mother said, toying with her pen. "I suggest you reflect upon our conversation this evening. Should you wish to speak with me further about anything, please don't hesitate. Now I wish you good night. I'll see you at Mass tomorrow." Sudden gusts slammed the windows behind her.

Later within the shadowy chapel, the darkened stained-glass windows looming around me, I knelt, my cheeks still inflamed. The solitary sanctuary lamp flickering over the tabernacle drew my gaze. Suddenly a blinding Light consumed me. Again, I was on fire, the ecstasy, wordless, like that morning of my First Holy Communion. Fresh tears erupted. "Yes, I'll do it," I gulped. "I'll ask to join the Society!"

Within the week, Reverend Mother McCabe, then Vicar of the Southern Vicariate, had accepted me for the postulancy in their noviceship in Albany, New York, the following September. Only later did I tell my parents. Both were shocked and teary-eyed but willing to support my decision. Other than a great-aunt I never knew, no one in the Costigan or Moloney families had ever embraced religious life. Such vocations bestowed great honor upon the parents.

Zipping up my black velvet sheath, its scoop neck and short sleeves banded in black satin, I felt like an imposter in my svelte body, a body like Mother used to have, as seen in photos taken when she was dating Dad. Unlike her, however, I would not have an earthly mate.

The doorbell rang. It was Joe.

Quickly, I fastened pearls around my neck, slipped on suede pumps, and rushed to the top of our circular steps to await Mother's announcement of Joe in our front hall, just as I had the evening of our first date. "You must not let him think you're too anxious to be with him," she had said, advice her Mother had given her, when a teenager. "Keep him waiting!"

I descended the stairs, slowly, Joe's eyes again sucking me into his fiery world. He was even more handsome than last summer, his wide grin stretching the corners of his mouth. "Hi, Liz," he said, breathing heavily upon my neck while helping me into my black velvet fitted coat, sewn by another seamstress. The gilt-framed mirror caught our fused passions. I lowered my eyes, fumbled with my kid gloves.

The rest of the evening blurred within surreal sound bites: Joe's adjustment to civilian life shared during the ride to the party, his hand reaching for mine across the seat; chatter, loud music, cigarette smoke, beer and wine in my friend's home; the seclusion of the kitchen and more of Joe's plans to work with his father in the B. Herder Book Company. All the while he toyed with my fingers, studied my newly sculpted body in black velvet. I listened, as always, furtively checking my watch for an acceptable time to return home and tell Joe my plan.

Elizabeth

We parked outside my back door, the porch fixture shadowing Joe's intense eyes, his cashmere muffler tucked in his overcoat, his hands sleek in leather gloves. Unlike that January night years before, I sat stiffly, staring at icy winds feathering snow upon the windshield. Joe moved closer, rested his arm upon my shoulders. I froze. I had to stop what was surely coming. "Joe, there's something you must know." A grimace creased his full lips. "There's been a change. I couldn't tell you in my letter."

"What change, Liz? Is there someone else?" His back stiffened.

"No, not that. This is so hard to say—this change—well, it's about my vocation—you know I've always been drawn to God." He nodded, speechless. I went on. "Several months ago, I had this experience during prayer—I'm supposed to become a nun."

Joe gasped, dropped his arm behind my seat.

"I've been accepted into the Kenwood noviceship in Albany," I continued in hesitant tones, gripping my gloved hands. "On Mary's birthday next September, I'll become a postulant, then begin my training to become a Mother." Shocked, he fumbled with a cigarette, inhaled deeply, stared into the shadowy darkness of the backyard. "After six months if I'm found suitable, I'll receive the white veil and habit of a novice. Joe, please try to understand. You mean a great deal to me. But this is something I must do."

He swiped at his eyes with his handkerchief, startlingly white in the gloom of the car. The longest silence of my life followed, until he asked, "Liz, can we still get together now and then before you leave?"

I nodded but knew I didn't mean it. No kiss at the back door. Inside our dim kitchen, I locked the door behind the only man who had ever loved me and trudged up the back stairs to my room.

Black Velvet Sheath, December 1956

Thus the blackness of my velvet sheath became a prelude to the blackness of the Society's habit I would later wear in the noviceship: the former, to seduce a mate; the latter, to embrace death before I had died. Only the trousseau list the Vicar had given my parents the afternoon of our visit afforded clues to life behind the cloister doors. I would experience that after entering. Years later, I saw this as an escape from Mother's designs for a future like hers, and from Joe's ardor, still too much for me handle. In my heart of hearts, I was still terrified of men, a secret I kept to myself.

5

Ivory Silk Taffeta Wedding Gown, March 17, 1958

"This is the day the Lord has made!" exclaimed the novice waking me in my curtained alcove in the noviceship dormitory. As required, I slipped to my knees, kissed the floor, responded in wispy tones, "Let us be glad and rejoice in it!" In a short while, dressed in the bridal gown Mother had selected before I entered Kenwood, I would become a true bride of Christ during the Mass of Clothing, and then be clothed as a novice in the Society of the Sacred Heart. My postulant days were over. I was twenty-two years old.

"There she is!" Mother exclaimed as I stepped through the pocket doors into the short parlor, holding my train. "How beautiful you are! Your gown—your veil—I don't know what to say!" Her response threw me. During the tense afternoon we'd selected this gown at Famous-Barr rather than a pricey one at Montaldo's, her words had been very different. Now she reached for me, hugged me hard, and her fur cape brushed my cheek.

Ivory Silk Taffeta Wedding Gown, March 17, 1958

Never had she shown such affection. The modesty veil on her felt hat could not conceal her tears. Other postulants, also dressed as brides, scrambled into the arms of loved ones around the parlor. Excitement bristled, flashes from cameras were reflected in gilt-framed mirrors on the walls and in tall windows framed with damask draperies. Outside, the sun shimmered upon towering blue spruces and maples, their limbs powdered with fresh snow.

Dad flushed, furtively studying my Child of Mary medal affixed to a white ribbon around my neck as he held my hand. "Happy St. Patrick's Day, Liz! Like my new tie with the clay pipes?" he said, leaning over and brushing the side of my cheek with a kiss. I froze, then stepped backward, blinking hard into his hesitant smile. "Sure is cold in Albany," he added. "No signs of spring here. In St. Louis, the forsythias are already blooming."

Behind him stood my brother Tom, a Holy Cross graduate, smitten by the blonde he would marry the following year; my sister Martha, a college junior and no longer a tomboy; and my maternal grandmother and two great-aunts, bleary-eyed from their overnight train ride to Albany. Their expressions bespoke joy and puzzlement: joy in my being clothed as a novice and desirous of first vows, puzzlement at this radical way of living out the Catholic faith. Staunch in their practice for decades, they never dreamed one of theirs would take such a drastic step. Yet they basked in my special call that redounded upon them.

"Let's get some pictures, quickly! There's not much time!" Mother said, her voice hardening. "I'm not supposed to take any in the chapel. Liz, you stand over there. I want one of you by yourself, then with the others. Hurry now!" She opened her Polaroid camera, checked the exposure. "Now, with my mother—then with Gussie and Blanche," she said. Dread tinged with merriment

33

flash-froze everyone posing with me. The finished pictures showed an ecstatic bride of Christ and her proud family. Soon, however, I would become someone else.

"It's time, Sisters," a shrill voice sounded through the commotion. "Tell your loved ones goodbye. They'll see you as novices after the ceremony." Disoriented by conversations dinning around me, I felt everyone hug me, hard, then release me to the unknown. Behind me, sobs broke out. I could not turn around.

Robot-like, I followed the other brides into the polished corridor and took my place in line outside the Kenwood chapel for the Mass of Clothing. Like the seven-year-old "little bride" of Christ, also veiled and dressed in white, the morning of my First Holy Communion at Our Lady of Lourdes Church, I was voiceless, subdued. Then as now, I felt like a doll with a painted smile.

While waiting for the signal to enter the Gothic chapel with the others, highlights from my postulancy jarred me: the first time I met Mother Schroen, the Mistress of Novices, my new mother, in the noviceship gardens the steamy afternoon I entered; the first time I observed everyone practicing custody of the eyes; the first time I saw the dormitories that slept twenty postulants and novices, devoid of all comforts; the first time I learned about the rule of silence that, except for rare holidays, forbade speaking outside of evening recreations presided over by Mother Schroen; the first time I learned hand signals during hurried meals in the monastic refectory; the first time I learned about the rule of cloister that outlawed leaving the convent's gated grounds; the first time I experienced the tinkling bell propelling more than ninety postulants and novices to each activity, from sunup to sundown, on the Order of Day posted outside Mother's office; the first time I'd sat mending a brown stocking in the noviceship room listening to Mother give Exercise, or instruction on the holy Rule; the first time I'd mopped corridors, scrubbed stairs, polished brass door handles, stitched in the workroom, peeled potatoes in the pantry, and dusted the dustless chapel; the first time I used Birdseye towels instead of Kotex; the first time I noticed postulants and novices being sent home by Mother; the first time I wore the spiked bracelet on my upper arm for four hours beneath my red blazer; the first time I had a refectory penance; the first time ill, alone in the infirmary in a real bed for two whole days; the first time one of the Mothers died, followed by the Office for the Dead, her solemn funeral Mass and burial in the cemetery at the top of a winding hill; the first time I received my mother's sheet cake for my twenty-second birthday, sent from an Albany bakery; the first Christmas with Mother's gifts for the noviceship, but no gifts for me. With the other postulants, I was practicing the vow of poverty and hated it.

Careful to avoid Mother Schroen's sharp tongue, I had repressed many other firsts and hid out among other postulants and novices. Assigned to the workroom, mornings and afternoons I stitched cache numbers on the clothing of incoming postulants and gloried in the yellowing of the great gingko tree outside the windows; it alone sustained the faint life-spark within me.

Suddenly, a sneeze twitched my nose. With my gloved hand, I stifled it, then wiggled my toes in my white flats. I was supposed to be a happy bride of Christ.

Organ music swelled from the choir loft. Families still whispered, swallowed sobs, and poured into the chapel, all ablaze with light. Vases of white carnations and roses and triple-branched candelabra adorned the marble altar; above it, a mural of the Sacred Heart, His arms outstretched in welcome. Many afternoons during adoration with the novices and postulants, I had collapsed into those arms and was solaced, just as I had been as a child.

Hearing the signal to move, I lowered my eyes and walked slowly down the long aisle, my hoopskirt and crinolines rustling about my feet. Then and for long years afterwards, I continued following others. On my own, I never knew where to go. In the sanctuary stood the Jesuit celebrant, Father Keenan, wearing a gold cope, and two altar boys.

Like a mechanical doll, I felt my legs propelling me closer to the steps of the communion rail for the first part of the ceremony. Picking up my skirts, I then knelt with the other brides. We were nine. (Eight others who'd entered with us last September had returned home. I, too, had yearned to be free from this harsh lifestyle but had nowhere to go. Besides, what would my family say, especially Mother, whose weekly letters glowed with new affection?) Prayers and censing the new novice veils followed. Then Mother Schroen began pinning long white novice veils over the lace veils of the others while the priest blessed them. Then it was my turn. Quickly, it was done. I was still a doll, but now in the hands of my new Mother who always wore black, her body tense as my mother's used to be, her words caustic. Much later, I learned they were the same age.

Numb, I went out of the chapel with the others toward the long parlor, as directed, while the organ played quiet interludes. Only twenty minutes in my ivory silk taffeta gown with a Sabrina neckline, an embroidered veil affixed to the Juliet cap; last week, ten minutes in front of the convent photographer in this splendid finery. What would come next?

I soon found out. Two professed Mothers took me in tow, led me to my new black clothing identified by my cache number, 64, and arranged on a sofa. More unseen hands removed my veils, casting them out of the way, then unbuttoned my gown, and within seconds, it was in a heap around my ankles, together with the hoop skirt and crinolines.

"Sister Moloney, come over here. Sit down and pull off your nylons. Put these on," a harried voice said. I noted her profession ring on her blunt finger, swallowed hard, and fastened black cotton stockings to loops on my girdle. In front of me, my new white flats were tossed aside for the new black oxfords I tied to my feet, purchased from Clark's the morning Mother and I had shopped for my trousseau.

"Stand up and unhook that thing around your waist." (It was the waist cincher, without which the gown would not have fit. My weight had ballooned, this time with the starchy diet of the convent.) "Your bra, too," the harried voice said again. I did so and felt the chill from drafty windows behind me. A softer voice across from me said, "Lift your arms over your head into these sleeves." It was the cotton chemise, a box-like garment I had secretly noticed during my afternoon employment in the workroom. Shivering, I pulled it down to my knees, fumbled with the drawstrings at the neck, and waited.

"Step into this petticoat," the harried voice said. It felt snug, buttoned around my waist. It was black, floor-length, a deep pocket on each side stitched to the waist. Muffled sighs surrounded me; other brides were also morphing into novices.

"Now sit down," the harried voice said. I felt a towel draped over my shoulders, heard the whack of the shears, saw thick brunette curls tumble into my lap. I shut my eyes, silently screamed for my lustrous hair. Nearby, other shears cut away.

"Now stand up," the soft voice said. Crisscrossing my chest now was a fichu, a white triangular cloth placed around my neck, affixed to loops on each side of my petticoat. Over all of this came the long black habit, fastened up the front with hooks and eyes. "And now the pelerine. Button it all the way up to your neck," the soft voice whispered. Upon my shoulders, I felt its weight; on my left side, invisible hands hooked large sidebeads through brass loops on my habit.

"Sit down," the harried voice said again, wearied by her task. I crouched again on the stool and felt the drawstrings of a white undercap fitting the contours of my newly shorn head. Next came a black grosgrain band tied across my forehead, then the starched cap. Hands placed it on the crown of my head, its fluted edges framing my face. More drawstrings, pulled from the nape of my neck, kept the cap in place. My temples shivered as chilly fingers pinned a long white veil to the cap.

"Sister, since Mass is a formal event, everyone unfolds their sleeves," the soft voice said. As I was following this directive, she pulled aside my veil, began slipping a black floor-length choir cloak over my shoulders. "Now stand up. You'll wear this in the chapel except during summer months. Like we all do." While fastening it at my neck, she said, beaming, "Sister Moloney, now you're beginning to look like a novice. Don't you agree?" she said to her helper, who nodded and was already bunching my bridal attire in her arms to dispose of it somewhere. Much later I learned the fabric from my bridal gown had been fashioned into a set of vestments for a missionary priest in South America.

"Sisters, take your places in the corridor for Mass," the shrill voice said again. Crazed by excitement, my glasses filming, I clumped in my new shoes, my heels already sore. No longer could I recognize the new novice in front of me by her cowlick; the others resembled stiff penguins in black and white. Only our faces and necks showed. Then triumphant strains heralded our reentry into the chapel. Like a moving tent, I followed the others down the main aisle. An infant howled from somewhere.

Then Father Keenan, a white chasuble defining his stooped shoulders, began the Latin prayers of the Mass. His solemn tone sucked me further into this drama. Despite the chill in the chapel, perspiration soaked my body; the baking soda did not stanch my underarm odor. My head pounded in unison with the hymns, prayers, the sermon about the Son of God incarnating/ clothing himself as Jesus of Nazareth. As His new brides, we were preparing for a similar immolation through our vows of poverty, chastity, and obedience that we would take after more formation. Passion for becoming His spouse, poor, humbled, and crucified, fueled this austere lifestyle, or so I believed at the time.

I sucked my dry teeth and fretted. The time for communion approached. My starched cap pinched my chin. Not sure where my mouth was, I knew I had to open it wide enough to receive the sacred Host. Somehow I did. Then maneuvering in long skirts, I made it back to my white *prie-dieu*, my inner world sucked into barrenness. No blinding Light to console me, to affirm this strange life path I was following. I gasped, gripped my hands, totally lost.

More hymns and prayers deepened my stupor. Following the priest's blessing, the choir intoned the *Magnificat*, swelling the chapel with explosive energy. It was time for the Kiss of Peace, an embrace of shalom, from hundreds of black-cloaked sisters standing in choir stalls on both sides of the chapel. While singing in the choir during other clothing ceremonies, I had longed for the time I would experience my own. But this was surreal. In a blur I followed the others up and down the aisles, astounded by strange joy flashing from somber faces within starched caps. Tears stung my eyes as the procession left the chapel, the corridor illumined by more flashbulbs.

Elizabeth

Then I met Mother, still wiping her eyes with her lace handkerchief. She pressed into my hand a new pocket watch, to be safety-pinned under my pelerine. Novices did not wear wristwatches, she had learned from the Vicar in St. Louis who had fast become her confidant. Mother's tears excited mine, our pending separation knifing our hearts. Dad's brown eyes glistened, words choking in his throat. More flashbulbs stunned me into deeper voicelessness and exhaustion as I pushed through the cloister doors and hurried downstairs to the refectory for my first dinner as a novice. I had to adjust.

In retrospect, the elegant world of my ivory silk taffeta gown became a bittersweet memory, while my novice habit became the metaphor for my living death between two Mothers from which there seemed no escape: my mother's unexpected attention in warm letters received every Wednesday and holiday sheet cakes for the combined noviceship and professed community; and Mother Schroen's cold demeanor, sharp words, and occasional hilarity when reading *Winnie-the-Pooh* or *Tommasina* during evening recreations. I dared not disappoint either mother. My black habit and white veil masked this insanity, even from myself. Thus I slavishly obeyed the tinkling bell summoning me and ninety other novices toward first vows of poverty, chastity, and obedience. Only when seated on the commode, locked in a stall in the common bathroom, was I alone.

6

Black Knitted Scarf,
1960–1965

"In the name of the Father, and of the Son, and of the Holy Spirit, and for the greater glory of the Sacred Hearts of Jesus and Mary, I, Mary Elizabeth Moloney, humbly prostrate...," More words flew off my tongue from the vow formula printed on the card I was holding; they were not mine. Two years had passed. It was again the feast of St. Patrick, the morning of my first vows in the Kenwood chapel, still redolent of the incense used in blessing our black veils and vow crucifixes at the beginning of Mass. We were now six. In front of me again stood Father Keenan, vested in white, holding the sacred Host before me. Behind me, my parents and other families knelt in the pews; the Mothers responsible for my formation, and the combined noviceship and professed communities, were in the choir stalls flanking the chapel. Somehow, I finished reading the vow formula and received the sacred Host on my tongue, then shut my eyes and listened to others pronounce vows of poverty, chastity, and obedience in confident tones.

Elizabeth

Kneeling again on my *prie-dieu* in front of the sanctuary with the others, our tall candles flaming above us—the same candles heading the pine coffins of our nuns' remains during funeral Masses—I buried my face in my hands. Again, no blinding Light. I was now dead to the world, an aspirant in the Society of the Sacred Heart. How had this come about? Often, I returned to last month's meeting with Mother Schroen, realizing I had pleased her, despite having no idea what I wanted for myself.

"Come in, Sister Moloney! I'm delighted to see you, my child!" exclaimed Mother Schroen, as she sat at her desk, illumined solely by a gooseneck lamp. Behind her, blustery winds imprinted snow swirls upon the bare windows. Above her, a Raphael Madonna hung on the wall. "Come! No need to kneel. Sit in that chair," she said. "Do you know why I wanted to see you this afternoon?"

I did but shook my head, taken aback by her unusual sweetness. I was approaching first vows, having almost completed two years of training as a novice.

"My child, you look pale! You've been drinking extra water, haven't you? Like the infirmarian told you?" I nodded, but still suffered from constipation. Never was there time to chew my food during meals in the refectory, nor time on the Order of Day for a proper evacuation.

Mother sat tall, her fingers plying her handwork, as she added, "Sister, you've done very well here. Over the years, I've picked up your eagerness to adapt to our ways as a postulant, your willingness to steep yourself in prayer and sacrificial practices as a first-year novice, your acceptance of humiliations rained upon you by Mother O'Rourke this year." I flinched, remembering the evening I had fled to an empty alcove in one of the dormitories and pounded piles of mattresses, my tears and snot besmirching the ticking. Had I been found out, I would have been sent home. But when the tinkling bell sounded for supper, I dried my eyes and raced down the darkened stairs to join the other novices and postulants. Again I blended in with the others, conforming their lives to the Order of Day, seen as the expression of God's will.

"Yes, I know all about your poor grades in elementary teaching methods. Mother O'Rourke told me. You're not cut out to be a teacher. We'll have other work for you. Our convents have many needs," Mother added, her bead-black eyes softening.

I wasn't sure where all this was going. Again I half-smiled, nodded, my inner world churning like whitecaps whipped by trickster winds.

Leaning over, she took my hands in hers and added, "Sister, these hands express your willing heart, grown large with desire to become a spouse of the Sacred Heart. To become one of us with first vows."

Still words failed me.

Slowly, Mother released my hands and scrutinized my soul. I squirmed against the small chair, distracted by winds hurling snowdrifts upon the noviceship terraces. That would mean more shoveling tomorrow, heavy work that Eddie Johnson, our garage man at home, had always taken care of. Only at Kenwood had I learned how to use a snow shovel, a rake, a broom, a mop, and I hated every minute of it.

"Yes, Sister, you've grown considerably since that hot September afternoon you arrived at Kenwood with your parents. Back then, I wondered if you'd make it, but then I saw you play field hockey the following week. As fullback, you repeatedly stopped the advancing forward line and shot the ball back to your postulant team. You have a strong will, Sister, once you know what's expected of you. That same eagerness to learn has brought you to this day," Mother said, smiling, her silky black veil meandering over one shoulder. "But there's not much more you can learn here. Reverend Mother and I believe you're sufficiently prepared to move toward first vows in the Society. On March 17, the feast of St. Patrick. Will you join us?"

My breathing looped within me. I wanted to bolt and run, but where would I go? Mother's eyes clouded.

"Sister, it seems like you need time. Know that we invite you to become an aspirant in the Society, should you wish to join us. Then another five years of formation before final profession at the motherhouse, if God so wills."

Suddenly I found words. "Yes, Mother, I'm thrilled. Something I've always wanted."

"Good, we're delighted!" Mother said, her face beaming as she took up her handwork. "Even though it's Lent, write your parents. Let them know. I'm sure they'll want to come for the ceremony."

That's how it happened.

Suddenly, everyone was standing for the celebrant's blessing. The Mass was ending. I stood in my new black oxfords, crossed myself, then grabbed my vow crucifix and followed the others for the Kiss of Peace from the community. My glasses fogged receiving their heartfelt wishes, hundreds of them. Even Mother O'Rourke, resembling a weathered old crow, grinned. I finally belonged to the Society.

As we moved outside the chapel, flashbulbs exploded, families smiled through their tears and reached for their black-veiled daughters. In the commotion, I felt Mother's hand on my arm and turned around. I still could not see very well. "Liz, we're so proud of you!" she exclaimed, pulling me close to her. Dad, all smiles, stood at her elbow, his trench coat opened to his brown suit, sporting another St. Patrick's Day tie. "This time, we get to visit with you after lunch," Mother added. "So much to tell you!"

Other new aspirants and their families, grouped in clusters beneath heavily draped tall windows, were already in the long parlor when I arrived. The din was terrible. I shuddered. With the rule of silence behind cloister doors, I was not used to talking. Bleary-eyed in my new black silk veil that tickled the bristles on my shaved neck, I spotted my parents seated upon a horsehair sofa in the far corner. After effusive greetings and more pictures, Mother pulled up a straight-backed chair for me and we sat down. I smoothed the knife-pleats of my new habit around me, then sat up straight and folded my hands. I pretended to be a happy aspirant. It was expected of me.

"Just look at you, Liz. You're so beautiful in that black veil!" Mother said. "The shots I just took of you just don't do you justice." I smiled and folded in my lap my swollen hands, the first evidence of rheumatoid arthritis that would play havoc with my body for the rest of my life. My glasses steamed under Dad's gaze as he lit a cigarette and continued studying me.

Then Mother reached for a floppy bundle wrapped in gold paper and ribbon that was next to her on the sofa, and handed it to me. Her blue eyes widened in anticipation, her voice expanded in deep joy. "Liz, I hope you like it—I had only one month to knit it. From the time I received your letter—I knitted everywhere, even the beauty parlor. You can imagine how pleased I was to tell others what I was knitting, a black scarf for you to wear on cold days once you became an aspirant with a black veil—I think I've got that right," she added, breathing deeply. "That's what the Vicar told me."

She was right.

I pulled apart the wrappings and spread the scarf on my lap. My heart dropped when I saw the plain stitches. I'd have preferred one with more design, like those I'd seen other aspirants and the professed wearing during walks outdoors for the noon examen. So strong was this desire, it obscured the vow of poverty I'd just taken. Stripped of all material goods, I was supposed to depend upon God's perfect providence through the Society to provide for all my needs. Only with the Superior's permission could I use gifts from my family, like this scarf.

Yet Mother still wanted to dress me.

"Thanks, Mother," I said, squelching my feelings. "You've always anticipated my needs—and now with this scarf. Each time I pin it under my cap, I'll pray for you. We've long winters here in Albany." She smiled deeply, her eyes glistening.

Covertly checking Dad's wristwatch, I kept track of the quarter hours before their departure for the airport. My smile began to ache, listening to Mother narrate family news already described in her weekly letters: my brother Tom had recently married and expected his first baby; my sister Martha was graduating from Maryville College; it was John's last year at St. Louis University High School; and how my youngest brother Mark's giftedness gave her trouble in finding a suitable school. "He's only eight now," she said, a frown creasing her forehead. "But he talks like an adult. Even acts like one. He's hard to manage. Before we left, he surprised us with a cake he'd baked, from scratch—we're thinking of getting him tested."

I nodded, crossed my feet under my skirts. Mother had still more to say. How she had disposed of my belongings, now that my vocation to the Society seemed settled with first vows. I wondered about that black velvet sheath, my gown for the Veiled

Prophet Ball, but said nothing. My diamond dinner ring, a ring first given to her by her parents when she graduated from Visitation Academy, she had placed in her safe deposit box.

No mention of the whispery tone in which I had recited my first vows, unlike the booming voices of the others kneeling next to me at the communion rail.

Then Mother Schroen, all smiles, her step lightsome, began circulating among the new aspirants and their families. "Mary! Tom!" she said, as she extended her slim hand to my parents, just as she had that humid September afternoon when I had entered the noviceship. "So good to see you again! You must be pleased with Liz. She's done very well with us. Like you, she has a generous heart. She'll only go far."

"We expect she will," Mother said fidgeting with her purse, unsure how to respond to this nun's ebullience. Dad, too, was miffed. During an earlier parlor visit, after having been named a Knight of Malta, he'd offered her a handkerchief with words stitched in blue at the top: "I'm the boss!" She frowned, stuffed it in her pocket, and left abruptly for the cloister.

I squirmed listening to the two Mothers, both fifty-six years of age, talk about the brightness of my new life as an aspirant in the Society. I knew better, but said nothing, just hid behind my smile, now paining the corners of my mouth. After more pleasantries, Mother Schroen left us for another new aspirant and her family.

In the corridor the grandfather clock chimed three o'clock. My parents stirred. It was time for them to leave.

With heavy steps, my parents accompanied me down the corridor toward the cloister doors. I dreaded their leaving, dreaded tomorrow's move to the aspirants' dormitory in the convent, dreaded yet another stern superior ready to continue my formation as a first-year aspirant, dreaded my newly vowed life among sixty nuns in the adjoining convent, many of whom were teachers in our Academy. Clutching the scarf Mother Schroen had given me permission to use, I turned and thanked Mother. She began to cry as she reached out for me, but my starched cap prevented her from getting close. Dad steadied her arm, his brown eyes also misting. Desperate to end this madness, I pushed open the cloister doors that swallowed me into more unknowns.

And there were many: the continuing breakdown of my body, mindless observance of the Rule, Mother's weekly letters that lured me into her comfortable world, studies toward my master's degree in English and the excitement of Gerard Manley Hopkins's poetry, transfer to St. Louis and Villa Duchesne in 1961 and classes teaching ninth-graders, and more parlor visits with my parents and their gifts for our community, now numbering thirty-three.

Thus my black scarf became a metaphor of my dependence upon Mother's care, afforded me in my mid-twenties, when supposedly I had a clearly defined life path: to live the triple vows taken in the Kenwood chapel and to deepen their practice for another five years before being approved for final vows at the motherhouse in Rome, Italy. I still yearned for Mother's support to buffer the harsh lifestyle behind the cloister doors.

Aside from this drama, another raged within the Catholic Church beyond our gated grounds. In October 1962, following three years of preparation, Pope John XXIII had convened the Second Vatican Council in St. Peter's Basilica, an effort to modernize the Catholic Church; its fever would undermine centuries-old beliefs and practices.

7

Black Leather Pouch, February 1965

Evening recreations, presided over by Reverend Mother Lamy, a seasoned woman of mirth, had buzzed with changes from the Second Vatican Council, nuanced from daily newspaper clippings that Reverend Mother's assistant placed on the community room table. (The rule of cloister forbade newspapers, radios, and television, seen as intrusive to our practice of contemplative prayer.) Fatigued by the day's work, I half-listened while mending torn stockings or anticipating a sweet from the candy box. However, the Council Fathers' publication of *The Sacred Constitution on the Liturgy* in 1963 and *The Dogmatic Constitution on the Church* in 1964 did impress me. Both radically changed the Catholic Church's practices of worship and self-understanding. Thus I was able to assuage some of Mother's concerns during parlor visits on Sunday afternoons. Dad's brown eyes smiled in a vacant way as he inhaled his cigarette and tried to follow the conversation.

However, the stress of maintaining allegiance to two mothers, my own and the Superior, the nutritionally deficient diet, chronic exhaustion and constipation, the lack of privacy—all weighted my spirit and continued destroying my knee joints and inflaming my hands. Lest I be found unsuitable for the Society and sent home, I said nothing. There I could not go, despite not knowing why. It was all a muddle. Eventually, I quit wearing the spiked bracelet on my upper arm and whipping myself, forty strokes, three times each week, in union with the passion of Jesus, practiced from the time I was a postulant.

Yet the Mother General of the Society, Reverend Mother Sabine DeValon, together with information provided by my Superiors, did approve me for the February probation, or final formation, at the motherhouse in Rome, Italy, in 1965.

The afternoon before my flight, my parents visited me in the heavily brocaded blue parlor at Villa Duchesne. Around us, casement windows opened to towering oaks, motionless, beneath brilliant skies.

"Mother! Dad! Such a surprise! It's not Sunday," I exclaimed, rushing into the parlor, despite stiff knees. "How good of you to come!"

"Reverend Mother said we could," Mother said, her blue eyes flashing with excitement. "Besides, we wanted to bring you this gift. Something for your trip," she added, handing me a black leather pouch with a shoulder strap. Dad looked on and smiled, tossed his overcoat over the sofa, then joined us.

"It's perfect!" I said, smoothing my hand over the soft leather, so unlike the pasteboard suitcase, bought for my entrance into the noviceship.

The rustle of sidebeads in the corridor alerted us to another visitor. It was Reverend Mother Lamy loping into the parlor, her black veil flowing behind her. Unlike most of my superiors in the Society, she was wise: a caring woman who laughed heartily and cried deeply; with unusual grace, she oversaw her nuns anxious about changes coming to the Society.

How she had chuckled after I criticized our New Year ritual honoring Jesus's birthday: processing into the chapel and singing carols, laying gifts before the poinsettia-banked crèche, followed by more prayer and carols. Still on my knees by her desk, I was perplexed. I'd expected her correction and refectory penance. "Sister Moloney, I couldn't agree with you more," Reverend Mother said after wiping her eyes and putting on her clear-framed glasses. "I've no idea when this ritual began or how it came about. It seems to mean a lot to the older nuns. That's why we do it. But with the renewal, there'll be many changes. Could still be a couple of years before that happens."

Before rising from my knees, I felt her bony finger trace the sign of the cross on my forehead, blessing me, her wide smile of crooked teeth heartening me. With her, I could almost breathe. Many times during spiritual direction, I had come close to revealing my divided world, but something held my tongue. Great was my need to appear the devoted aspirant, ever deepening my commitment to the Society. This attitude drew others' smiles and occasional winks that sustained me for another day within this harsh life.

"You must be so pleased by Liz's acceptance into probation!" Reverend Mother exclaimed to my parents after eyeing me fondly. "And supplying her with that handsome pouch. I know she'll have use for it," she added, smiling.

"We'd hoped so," Mother added, quickly wiping a tear besmirching her carefully rouged cheek. The afternoon sunlight revealed more streaks of grey in her brunette pageboy. More baldness lengthened Dad's forehead, ever tense as he looked on.

Again I felt trapped between my two mothers, both anticipating my future in the Society. In my heart of hearts, I still had no idea what I wanted for myself. But I did have a black leather pouch, my toehold in the comfortable Moloney world. I wanted more.

The next morning I finished packing the wool cape the vestiare had stitched for me to wear beneath my pelerine, "to fend off the dampness of the motherhouse," she said. Then I placed my Rule book, the *Jerusalem Bible*, and a new black binder for my reflections during probation in my pouch. I had no personal items. My toothbrush was in my suitcase.

The TWA flight was surreal: the cramped cabin, dim lighting, foul air, tasteless meals, chattering passengers moving up and down the aisles, a baby wailing. All the while, I felt the pouch at my feet and dreamed of my first ocean crossing on the *Americana* with my parents in 1952. Then, I had felt excited, protected; on this one, however, alone, filled with dread. Only at the last minute did swarthy guides show up at the airports, handle my suitcase and passport, and tell me where to go. When I deplaned at Rome's Fiumcino Airport, I discovered thirteen other American RSCJs on the same flight, most of whom I had not seen since Kenwood's summer school. Our tongues held by our rule of silence, we stood on the tarmac, huddled in our shawls against the damp chill, waiting for our driver from the motherhouse.

Bused to the Roman-Revival-style motherhouse, 117 Via Nomentana on the outskirts of Rome, I stared out from a frosted window. Everything blurred into everything else. This sensation plagued me during the next five months of probation within the heavily gated cloister, next to the Russian Embassy. Another Order of Day, similar to the Kenwood noviceship, hollowed me. Again my sole reprieve was the gardens, tended by green-smocked, balding workmen. With the flowering of forsythia, jonquils, the fruit trees, my spirit stirred, but only until called to the next employment within the motherhouse. Occasionally the mirth of Reverend Mother Melia, the Mistress of Probation, moved me.

Thus I was trapped in the hole of my own making and saw no way out. The stakes only mounted. My parents, siblings with spouses, two of my father's sisters, a great-aunt and two of her daughters, and an uncle all planned to attend my final profession in July, even accompany me on the voyage home on the *Michelangelo*. I paid little heed to my knees bloodied from scrubbing marble staircases and from long hours on wooden kneelers in the Gothic chapel. I disregarded my worsening limp, all the more since learning one of the South American probanists had left the Society.

Still in a blur, wearing a new habit and my Sunday shoes, I knelt with thirteen other American probanists in the motherhouse chapel. It was the stifling morning of my final profession, July 22, the feast day of St. Mary Magdalene. High drama bristled to the point of pain. To my right was Uncle Bill, partially hidden behind a column, filming this event despite its being forbidden. Dad's cigarette cough cued me to his presence and those of relatives kneeling behind me.

Prayers and hymns of the Mass followed predictably until the time came for our vows before the raised Host held by the

American Dominican, Father Boyle. We began in unison, my wispy voice carried by the others.

"In the name of the Father and of the Son and of the Holy Spirit..." I lost my breath, gulped for air, fingered the card with the vow formula. I looked around. Who were these young nuns embracing immolation, for life, within the Society of the Sacred Heart? What was I doing among them? My superiors had always said I fit in the Society. Maybe they were right. I fit nowhere else. "... humbly prostrate in the presence of the Most Holy Trinity, of the Most Holy Virgin Mother of God, of all the Heavenly court," my peers continued in unison. I listened, then joined them. "I promise to Almighty God, and to you Reverend Mother Sabine DeValon, our Superior General ...." Again I zoned out, perspiration filming my glasses. It was impossible to escape the momentum building around me. I had no choice but to participate. I managed to whisper, "... perpetual poverty, chastity and obedience, and according to obedience, to consecrate myself to the education of youth, in conformity to the Spirit of our Institute." From a faraway place, I heard the others conclude, "Under the authority of His Eminence Cardinal Aloysius Talia, Vicar General of His Holiness Pope Paul VI and of our ecclesiastical Superiors. Made at Rome, in the Chapel of our House of the Sacred Heart of Jesus, the twenty-second day of July, 1965."

It was done. After receiving communion, I clutched my new cross upon my sunken chest and fingered the silver ring on my right hand, evidence of final profession in the Society. I was truly dead to the world. I had to get used to it, despite hankering for the softer life of my parents. They must never know.

Jubilant organ strains enlivened the Kiss of Peace from the motherhouse community. With the last embrace from the Italian nun who had helped me during afternoons in the print shop, I followed the others to our families already clustered around the chapel doors. More flashbulbs, more pretending, followed. Legally a member of the Society of the Sacred Heart, I still did not belong. Then outdoors to tables set with orange drinks and shortbreads beneath the shade of bottleneck pines in the gardens. Still more picture-taking, more congratulations, more hugs, more small talk.

Nearby, another visitor fanned his face with his Panama hat and decried President Johnson's deployment of more troops to Vietnam, wherever that was. Then more well-wishes from Reverend Mother Melia, her dark eyes smiling behind Coke-bottle lenses. Soon the late morning heat forced my guests to their accommodations in the air-conditioned Grand Hotel with promises of more visits once aboard our ship.

That night, Dad invited the St. Louis contingent to a white-glove supper in one of the Grand Hotel's private rooms. On his left was an empty chair, my accustomed place in our dining room before I had entered the convent.

I dreaded returning to Villa Duchesne, to a new Superior, and more teaching. Still overlooked were years of failure in class-rooms with middle-schoolers, despite my master's degree in English. However, there would be parlor visits with Mother and Dad, and more gifts.

Overriding these concerns, however, loomed the final session of the Second Vatican Council and with it, the total revamping of the Church. Reverend Mother Melia had forewarned us about changes coming from the Sacred Congregation of Religious and Secular Affairs. As professed members in the Society with a vow of obedience, we must weather the upheavals, becoming more relevant to the needs of the modern world, whatever that meant.

But despite gnawing fears, I would learn to fill my black leather pouch with personal items, as I moved into ever-expanding worlds around me.

8

The Modified Habit,
March 1967

Uneasy beneath the persona of a new professed, I returned to Villa Duchesne in 1965 and plummeted into painful changes that curiously began my long and anguished emancipation from the Society, the first of many.

For the first time since entering the noviceship, I had no respect for my new superior, Reverend Mother Stanley, tall and stooped, her black veil enveloping a pear-shaped body. She reminded me of a broken windmill, a powerless hulk, its arms flailing in trickster winds. Like me, she had a wispy voice, often cleared her throat. Oblivious of my problems relating to children, she assigned me five classes in the high school, care of forty-seven boarding students, and assistant to Mother O'Meara, the Mistress General. It was believed my vow of obedience would sustain me. It did not. The insanity of this twenty-four-hours-a-day workload further enervated me. Parlor visits with my parents melded within the next duty, leaving me scant time for the divided life of my two mothers.

Elizabeth

After one year of this madness, Mother O'Meara sensed my turmoil and offered nightly counseling in her shadowy office after I'd put the boarders to bed. For the first time in my life, I found a real mother, her dark eyes inviting my confidence, and with tearful abandon, I blurted out stories of my childhood, Joe, my years in the Society, the pain in my joints. Night after night we shared. Her pelerine heaved with laughter, and within her laughter, I soon discovered my own.

But it was not all dark. Mother's recent return from studies on the Notre Dame campus with other sisters from different communities had exposed her to their renewal, mandated by the Vatican II's Decree on Renewal of Religious Life, *Perfectae Caritatis*, in August 1965. *The Norms*, as they were called, mandated semi-cloistered congregations with apostolic works, such as the Society of the Sacred Heart, to revamp their lifestyles, perceived as antiquated, in order to be more effective in their ministries. An emerging new theology of the vows also enhanced these changes. It was a heady time.

Her eyes flashing, Mother O'Meara shared stories of theologians presenting new paradigms that fueled experimentation among the sisters and priests, such as fraternizing during home Masses, drinking and smoking around the campus, modified habits, television and newspapers, and so much more. Mother assured me that our Society would also change. Preparations were already underway for a Special Chapter at the motherhouse sometime next year. Hope burned deep, lightened my steps. Even the children welcomed my hesitant smile. My parents also noted something different about me and liked it.

The 1966 Christmas break promised even more hours with Mother O'Meara and extra sleep. Or so I hoped. After straightening the chairs in my classroom and the study hall, I headed toward the refectory and my afternoon hot chocolate. From the chapel emerged Reverend Mother, her eyes hot coals of anger.

"Sister Moloney! Sister, dear! We must talk! Now!" she said, clutching her prayerbook against her chest, waiting for me to catch up with her. Never had I seen her so furious. Instead of moving to a "little words corner" in the basement, in observance of the rule of silence, she stood her ground in the empty corridor, her face purpling beneath her bandeau, her stooped shoulders towering over me.

"Sister, dear!" she said, "I've heard you and Mother O'Meara have been breaking greater silence! Those visits in her office must stop at once! I forbid you to see her! I'm your superior and available for all your needs!" I gasped, pressed my toes against the soles of my shoes. After clearing her throat, she continued, "We've also decided to replace you as Mother's assistant and surveillante of the boarding school. And you're to return to the aspirants' dormitory in the cloister immediately. When the children return in January, you'll continue teaching and help surveille study halls and recreations when needed. That will be all!" She turned abruptly and pushed through the cloister doors, banging behind her.

I was stunned. Again the angry mother of my childhood had cut me to the quick. Later recourse to Mother O'Meara was fruitless. "We have our obedience," she muttered, nervously fingering her profession ring, then turned back to her typing. Shut off from my life-source, I grabbed my shawl, pulled on my rubbers, tore outside, and huffed up the snow-packed road toward the gate, and then, like a caged animal, turned around and retraced my steps.

Elizabeth

After the children returned from the holidays in 1967, they noted my sullen expression in the classroom, in the corridors, but said nothing. Mother O'Meara remained distant, even during talking meals. My isolation increased. Even prayer hurt. There was no real sleep, only thrashings atop my bed, the Army blanket in knots around my feet.

Several months later, Reverend Mother Stanley skittered into the community room for recreation; in her large hands, she toyed with glossy photos.

"Sisters, I just heard from the motherhouse this morning," she said in strained tones, then cleared her throat. "You remember the *Norms of 1965*, about the modification of habits?" An uncanny silence gripped everyone, as she continued. "Our Mother General and her Assistants have decided we, too, must adopt a different style of habit." She paused, then looked at the semicircles of nuns seated before her. Faces whitened, needles poised in midair over torn stockings. Again clearing her throat, the Superior continued, "You know many communities around the world have modified their habits to be more approachable to God's people. We're to do similarly—these photos will give you an idea of what is to come." Older nuns moaned, studied the pleats in their skirts, wrung their hands; younger ones giggled. I shot a glance at Mother O'Meara, remembering the changes she had predicted during our nightly meetings in her office last year.

"Would you look at this?" Mother O'Meara roared, studying one of the photos. "Looks like no more petticoats, chemises, or fichus. No side beads. We'll probably have to wear bras and slips again. I thought I'd given them up years ago!" she added, rolling her expressive eyes. The room buzzed with the announcement of this first change in the Society—a long black habit with seamed pleats down the front and back, fastened by Velcro openings at the shoulders and a fabric belt at the waist.

"And no more starched caps!" Mother added, pulling hers over her square chin. "We'll be able to see out of the corners of our eyes again." The model in the photo wore a celluloid headband affixed to a cotton cap, covered by an opaque veil that fell just below her shoulders. As the photos were passed around, more exclamations and hangdog looks filled the room. Crazed by excitement, I crossed my knees, perceived as worldly in the Society.

When the din settled, Reverend Mother stretched tall in her Windsor chair and added, "Our vestiare will take everyone's measurements, starting tomorrow. Then we'll send them out to be made." Yet another windstorm cut short her remarks, whipped more hilarity among us; after it petered out, she added in strained tones, "We'll wear the modified habit for Easter Sunday Mass. Our vow of obedience will help us adjust to this change." For the remainder of recreation, everyone spoke out of turn, flummoxing Reverend Mother, reddening her squirrel-like cheeks. On the way to the chapel for Office and night prayers, whispers echoed in the corridor, the rule of silence barely able to restrain our tongues.

Months later, our modified habits bagged in plastic sleeves evoked titters like those of naughty children on holiday. Reverend Mother's reminders of silence could not squelch the flow, nor did she assign refectory penances, strangely a thing of the past. A force beyond our reckoning had a toehold in our cloistered life and would shake it to its foundations. More and more, I retreated to my inner world, my new habit hanging, unopened, on the back of the door of the aspirants' dormitory.

Palm Sunday afternoon, overcast, humid, I was visiting my parents in the blue parlor. With only a few minutes before the bell for benediction in the chapel, I froze sitting on my straight-backed chair.

"Hello, Mary! Tom!" It was Reverend Mother, all smiles, her hands folded at her waist. "So good to see you again! It's been a while."

We stood. My parents received her welcome, their strained smiles bespeaking annoyance.

"I suppose Liz has told you of our new habits we'll wear on Easter," Reverend Mother added. My parents looked at me, questioningly.

"Well, we'll fix that! Sister, dear, go upstairs and put on your new habit. Give your parents a preview. They'll enjoy that!" she said, grinning.

Not wanting to create a scene, I did as she said.

In my alcove, I slowly removed my worn habit, remembering the unseen hands of the Mothers who had clothed me as a novice at Kenwood years before, then withdrew the new habit from the plastic bag and figured out how to put it on. The same for the new headwear. With only my pocket mirror to guide me, I managed and made my way back to the parlor. Instead of feeling like a moving tent as I did in the old wool habit, the stiffness of the new one, a polyester blend, felt like a cardboard box.

"Sister, dear!" Reverend Mother exclaimed, standing outside the parlor with Mother O'Meara. "How lovely! That new habit becomes you! You wear it well!" I cringed, lowered my eyes, gripped my hands, hard.

"And such a waistline!" Mother O'Meara added, nurturing me in her warm gaze, one I'd not experienced for months, one I still hungered for. "Something I don't have," Reverend Mother quipped, fingering the sharp pleats of the pelerine that fell below her waist. Years of eating on the run, necessitated by her heavy responsibilities, had done their worst. A lemon-smile smarted on my lips at seeing Reverend Mother and Mother O'Meara together, frivolous and chatty. I rejoined my parents.

"Here she is! Isn't she lovely?" It was Reverend Mother again, this time exclaiming to my parents, clearly taken aback by my appearance. "Sister dear, turn around and let them see the back," she tittered. Mother O'Meara joined in. Fortunately the bell for benediction ended this madness, and I tore to my alcove to redress and join the choir. No more was said about the new habit.

Easter morning arrived, a resurrection of sorts. Furtive glimpses over the tops of our Office books and longer ones during Mass embarrassed our celebrant. Afterwards, a talking breakfast in the refectory sparked more commotion. Older nuns still grieved the old habit that had disguised poor posture, wrinkles, and sagging jowls; they squirmed in undergarments pinching in the wrong places. Younger ones sat tall, preening in their newly defined women's bodies. I was at odds with mine. Again, others had dressed me, this time, in the modified habit of the Society.

9

Play Clothes, Summer 1967

Despite my animosity toward Reverend Mother Stanley, she was instrumental in my later transfer to The Rosary, our twelve-grade academy founded in 1886, located on St. Charles Avenue in New Orleans. She had received a letter from the New Orleans Diocese describing an eight-week program in Central City, a government-designated poverty area, and suggested I volunteer. I had no summer plans. Since "solidarity with the poor," a key theme from the documents of the Vatican II renewal, had been drawing nuns and priests to ghettos across the country, I agreed. It would also give me reprieve from my "Sister, dear" superior and involve me in the world beyond our cloister gates.

On a sultry June morning I flew into New Orleans, and with my black pouch slung over my shoulder, headed toward the terminal. The noise was deafening, the air cloying. Someone from this diocesan program was to meet me.

"Hey! Are you Sister Moloney? I'm lookin' for Sister Moloney!" a raspy voice called behind me.

I turned around, then nodded, still nonplussed from the send-off at Villa Duchesne. Again Mother O'Meara had bathed me in her warm regard, as she pressed into my hands a notebook she'd made for my Central City experiences. She promised to write.

"I'm Sister Mary David! Come to meet you!" she said, thrusting her black veil over hefty shoulders. A short Dominican nun, her starched coif squeezed her flushed face and neck; salt-and-pepper eyebrows spilled atop clear-frame glasses slipping down her squat nose. "When I heard a Madame of the Sacred Heart was comin' to help us this summer, I nearly had a fit! Never heard of 'em helpin' po' folks!" Her mouth hardened into a thin line. Immediately, I was on the defensive as I followed her to the baggage carousel for my suitcase.

"Well, Sister David, many don't know that our foundress set up separate schools for poor and wealthy girls, often on the same grounds. In the eighteen-hundreds," I blurted, transferring my pouch to the other shoulder.

"I sure don't see any signs of that today. What brings you here?" she pressed.

After I explained, she snapped, "Sounds like you've no experience with the poor. Teachin' or otherwise."

"That's right. I've come to learn." Then in frosty silence we continued toward the baggage claim.

"Humph! 'Round here, they call me David. None of that Sister stuff!" she said, grabbing my suitcase from the carousel and taking off toward the station wagon, guarded by one of her police friends in a no-parking zone.

Ill-functioning vents in David's air-conditioned car worsened the dampness of my habit. I said nothing, cooking in my own juices, staring out the window. The long drive toward Central City was like a bad dream: blocks of sun-blistered shotgun houses with sagging stoops, vacant lots teeming with chicory and thistle, burnt-out trucks and litter lining the streets. Two mongrels copulated on the dusty sidewalk. St. Francis de Sales Parish on Second Street would be my home for the summer.

"This is it! St. Francis de Sales!" David said, slowing to a stop and parking. Across from me, a steeple loomed into the milky sky; beneath it, a frame church yellowing with age; next to it, the convent and boarded-up school with broken windows.

After leaving my bags in the convent, we joined the other nuns in the diocesan program for orientation at Notre Dame Seminary on Carrollton Avenue, a grassy complex of buff-colored build-ings, tastefully shrubbed and air-conditioned.

Later over the spaghetti supper David had prepared, I blinked back fatigue and studied the perspiring faces of my co-workers, from various communities whose habits were black, brown, or white. Their high-pitched chatter annoyed me. One wiped her forehead, pulled at the wimple around her neck, beamed through fleshy jowls, then said, "We're women of the Church, on the cusp of change! With our teaching backgrounds, we're bound to make a difference in the lives of these poor children!" Her companion exclaimed, "You're so right, Sister! Those presentations on Central City we heard this afternoon will surely help us under-stand them! The paraprofessionals seemed so knowledgeable! So welcoming!" Then a brown-habited nun chimed in, "Didn't you love Bishop Hannon's welcome, so cordial, so fatherly? We're in good hands!" Others grinned, raising questions about mutual acquaintances in other schools in the diocese, while slathering butter on chunks of Italian bread. I felt invisible, sloshing my feel-ings in red wine. Across the table, David suddenly winked at me.

"Hey, Moloney, you look overwhelmed! Too much for you to handle?" David said later, her white sleeves rolled to her elbows, her meaty hands plunged into soapy water. I nodded, standing next to her at the sink wiping dishes with a threadbare towel. "No sweat!" she said. "If you like, check in with me each evenin' and we can review your day." While stacking the dishes in the cupboard, I wondered about this nun, unexpectedly taking me under her expansive wing.

Later in the only bathroom, I looked into the silvering mirror while brushing my teeth, my mind racing: no privacy; no lock on the bathroom door; too many sisters in this cramped and noisy convent, barely cooled by second-hand window units; too hot and dangerous to walk outside; a wheezing roommate; the children, tomorrow.

The next morning fifty-five youngsters in all shades of brown slid onto student chairs in the parish school basement, silently staring at us, their faces glistening with perspiration. Especially uneasy was a boy who slipped off his sandal and picked at his sore toe.

"I'm Harold," he stammered under his breath, when I asked his name.

Next to him, two girls in starched sundresses giggled, covering their mouths.

"I'm Brenda," one said, twisting her braid around short fingers.

"I'm Stacy," the other said, looking at Brenda.

I wrote their names on my roster but could not understand many of the others. Perhaps they'd never seen nuns in habits.

Lessons in spelling, reading, and math floated upon stagnant air, massaged by the single government-leased fan atop a stool in the corner. Bricks propped storm doors, affording the only source of light. At intervals, I checked my watch, eyed my co-workers' frustration. They too were having a rough time. Promptly at noon, the children bolted, their shorts and dresses rumpled from squirming on their chairs. Their hoots suggested something we did not know.

Next door in the yellowing church the Folk Mass began, offered by the pastor, rotund in his green vestments. Large fans positioned around the altar whipped up years of dust coating the pews. Seminarians in black shirts with collars, also working in the parish, led us in Ray Repp songs while strumming twelve-string guitars. Soon the morning's fiasco morphed into the euphoria of the renewing Church, extending its mission to the recently discovered poor.

During a hasty lunch in the convent afterwards, few spoke.

After wolfing down a ham sandwich, I slung playground equipment over my shoulder, grabbed David's directions to the Guste Projects, my afternoon assignment, and headed for the bus stop. I needed no fare. As thanks to the Daughters of Charity for nursing yellow fever victims from 1848 to 1849, and later in 1878, the city fathers decreed that all nuns, hereafter, would ride free on public transportation. Blocks with withered oleander bushes whizzed past. Traffic was heavy. I got off at Simon Bolivar Avenue. Unnerved by honking cars, their emissions hazing the sun, I pressed ahead, studying the cracks in the sidewalk lest I trip. I wondered about the kids I'd meet, if they'd all look alike as they had earlier, if I'd understand them, if I'd lose my voice. Paraprofessionals were supposed to help me with the children.

Ahead, the Guste Projects loomed, three-story cinderblock buildings connected by breezeways; an asphalt neutral ground, shimmering under the heat, spanned their length. No grass or shrubs anywhere. Bordering the sidewalk was a solitary tree, and beneath its spotty shade lounged black women sipping Cokes, their sullen eyes stopping me in my tracks.

"Hello! I'm Sister Moloney from St. Francis de Sales. Are you the paraprofessionals I'm supposed to meet? To work with the kids this afternoon?" I said, dropping my equipment to the ground. The heavy-breasted woman in the polka-dot halter shifted on her elbow, grunted, and turned up the volume on her boom box. Others filed their nails, flayed me alive with glances like sharp daggers. Silenced, I gathered my stuff and headed toward the baseball diamond, outlined upon the baking asphalt. Nearby, timid girls stared at my long skirts and black veil, and reluctantly joined me. Our game began, accompanied by rock strains from the boom box.

"Hey, David, can we talk?" I asked uneasily, balancing myself upon a stool, while she stirred tomato sauce on the stove. A checkered apron spanned her girth, a colorful addition to her white habit.

"Moloney, good to see you!" Her bushy eyebrows rose in concern. "Grab that knife and chop up those vegetables. We're havin' the pastor for supper." Flipping her veil over her shoulder, she turned to the pan she was tending and added, "So you had your first day in the inner city. How'd it go?"

"Not well at all. Staring, voiceless kids in the morning. Not much better this afternoon," I said, lowering my eyes, then chopped stalks of celery. Little did David know that meal preparation was another first for me, as was the evening news filtering into the kitchen from the small black-and-white television in the living room. The upstairs commode flushed, the pipes groaned. After wiping perspiration from my forehead, I continued, "Some girls joined me for baseball for a while until the heat drove them home, to their soaps, I guess. And the so-called paraprofessionals just sat and stared at me." I gripped the handle of the knife. "And what's worse, I felt eyes from the surrounding buildings studying me the whole time. Of course, no one offered me a glass of water!"

"So, Moloney, what did you learn?" David asked, swiping at a fly zooming above the tomato sauce.

"Not sure I learned anything. I don't fit in here. I don't understand what anyone says. Am I the problem?"

"Not necessarily," David said, checking the pasta boiling in another pot. "I'm not so sure you didn't learn anythin'. Sounds like you picked up a lot—the prejudice between our races." She paused, studying my face. "Theirs was forged by centuries of misery and enslavement. We know only the facts. In no way can we understand what they went through. Yet they survived." She swiped a tear on her fleshy cheek with her handkerchief, then stuffed it in her side pocket. "But Dr. King is tellin' their story. It's finally bein' heard. But you've got to be attuned to it to pick it up. I work at it every day."

"But how do I attune myself to their world? I barely get along in the white one."

"Don't sweat, Moloney. It'll come. Have patience. You can't know how you influenced those you met today. Just give it your best shot tomorrow. I know you will." David winked, turned down the fire beneath the pan, checked her watch. "And get one of the others to help out! Father will be here soon."

Later, I retreated to the chapel, a closet-size room on the second floor with a belching air conditioner circulating frigid air. The sanctuary lamp next to the tabernacle flamed in the stuffy darkness, as I gripped my face in my hands and tried to pray. Nothing.

Days of unrelenting heat and frustration followed, bearable only through David's nightly support.

On the weekend, with no desire to return to The Rosary, or orders to do so, I joined David and some of the nuns at the screened-in estate of a wealthy benefactor in Covington, its timbered grounds affording seclusion and quiet. Besides resting, we were eager to experiment with alternative modes of living within the Vatican II renewal, as were many communities of nuns.

"After we've washed the dishes, come upstairs. I've got a surprise!" David grinned, her belly shaking with delight. The chardonnay we enjoyed with our barbecued chicken swam in my head.

"Now, gather 'round," she chuckled, slinging a battered suit-case upon the four-poster. Wild with anticipation, we watched. "Some things in here might interest you!" She popped open the lid, spilling play clothes of all colors onto the spread. "Folks gave us these to help with our renewal! If you wish, choose an outfit! No need to wear your hot habits here!" I wondered if anything would fit. It had been so long. When my turn came, I picked out a red shirt, plaid shorts, and sandals, then hurried to my room, its French doors opening onto a balcony with a polished verandah.

There I stood in front of a full-length mirror, startled by the whiteness of my hands, face, and neck, the rest of my body shrouded in black. With new resolve, I doffed my headband and veil and discovered chopped hair spiking like porcupine quills, the result of weekly trimmings with blunt scissors, weeks before. Then I removed my habit, tossed it on the bed, removed my undergarments, untied my oxfords, and pulled off my stockings, clothing I used to regard as sacred, now just smelly and worn. My fingers shook, buttoning the shirt, zipping up the shorts. Again, I looked into the mirror stunned by my reflection. Who was this looking back at me? What had happened to her body, her bare arms, her thick waistline, inflamed knees? Suddenly winded, I sat down and buckled sandals onto feet still blotched from laces tied too tightly.

"Hey, Sisters! What's takin' you so long?" From downstairs, David called. "Come to the family room and let's dance! I've got Herb Alpert's *Tijuana Brass*! And there's more wine, left over from supper!" Again I turned and looked into the mirror. My mouth was suddenly dry.

Holding onto the banister, I made my way to the paneled room, ablaze with lamps, their yellow glow softening my misgivings as I poured myself another glass of wine and looked around. My co-workers grinned sheepishly in their play clothes, sipped wine, lounged on over-stuffed armchairs. We all looked like rumpled bag ladies on holiday. Suddenly, Sister Marcella, a staid Ursuline nun, began to titter. Others joined in until the room rocked. "Let's dance!" David called, increasing the volume on the phonograph. Trumpets blared. Hot rhythms stirred my body. I was on my feet, dancing wildly, perhaps like those nuns and priests on the Notre Dame campus Mother O'Meara had described last year.

At sunrise I awoke in a fog, worsened by bird trills outside my French doors. Clutching my head, I leaned back upon the pillows, an unopened book of poems on my lap. Last night's laughter, dancing among new friends, the discovery of my body, the thrill of wearing the shirt and shorts and sandals, the mellowing effect of that second glass of wine—all befuddled me. Too much to sort out. I got up and put on my play clothes, my habit left in a heap on the dresser. I looked into the mirror and smiled. Red always looked stunning on me, as my mother had said long ago. Turning sideways, I felt my breasts and grinned. I still had them.

That afternoon my sandals crunched the pine-needle path bordering the estate, and a soft breeze lifted shorn hairs from my neck. I was free, achingly so, at least in that moment.

More grueling weeks followed, salved by weekends in our Covington getaway and David's nightly counsel.

"But where is all of this leading, David?" I asked after an especially hot day with the children. Again she was treating me to an oyster loaf sandwich at her favorite haunt, crowded with students and blue-collar workers. David and I had become fast friends, a glimmer of which I caught during orientation that first day at the seminary. Realizing I had no money on our lunch break at Burger King, she had whispered, "Hey, Moloney, get what you want. I'll cover it," so as not to embarrass me in front of the others. Never had I tasted such a hamburger; hungrily, I licked pickle relish and mayonnaise off my fingers, rather than use my paper napkin. The fries slid down my throat with the Coke. No one, not even David, seemed to notice my discomfort eating in public, having had meals only in our refectory the past ten years. In retrospect, we eleven nuns, all in varied habits, must have drawn whispers from other patrons seated around us.

"Well, where do you think it's takin' you? You're on your own path and willin' to learn. You sure don't shirk from hardships," David said, tucking a napkin under her chin to avoid staining her white scapular, her good blue eye quickened by my question. A matching glass eye filled the other socket, the result of a childhood accident, I later learned.

"But unlike you I still hate the stench of poverty—like death," I said. "Only running into Brenda, Harold, and Stacy most afternoons on my way home from the bus stop makes all this worthwhile." David listened, her blunt fingers tapping the corner of the menu. "And they were there this afternoon, their bare feet dancing on the hot sidewalk. Waving their melting popsicles and hollering as always, 'Ster Baloni! 'Ster Baloni! 'Ster Baloni! We's here! Comes to meet you!' Their fruity kisses tickled my chin, while I explained for the umpteenth time the correct pronunciation of my name. To which, they yelled even louder, giggling, 'Ster Baloni! 'Ster Baloni!' Harold grabbed the bats and gloves; the girls snatched my hands and paraded me toward the convent. I felt so honored."

David grinned. "There, you see, Moloney, that's what's this is all about! Love! With these kids, you've connected. Perhaps the major lesson of your summer in Central City."

"I never thought of it that way. But the afternoons I miss them, I'm sad." I lowered my head. "But I get even sadder thinking about the end of this program. You've taught me so much about life. How our neighbors survive."

Especially was this true the night screeching sirens and red lights tore us from sleep. After throwing on my habit, I climbed into David's station wagon and we sped down Second Street, drawn by acrid smells to the next block. There, galloping flames consumed the shotgun house, its distraught homeless hugged by neighbors. I watched as David shot commands to the fire marshal, another friend of hers. She knew what to do.

Distracted by a telecaster analyzing the recent riots in Detroit and Newark, citing numbers killed or injured and property damaged, David then wiped her sticky hands on her napkin and asked, "Remember that night we waited out the rumor of Dryads Street burning, with the bishop and seminarians?" I nodded. We had remembered that many times afterwards.

"Things are still explosive. Here and all over our country!" She studied me hard, her mouth a grim line. "Moloney, what does all this mean if you're studying library science in Washington, D.C., next month? Sounds like a cop-out to me!"

"David, I already told you. Last winter Reverend Mother Stanley had me tested, and the results showed an aptitude for library science. Before I knew it, I was signed up at Catholic University and our convent nearby. I didn't agree but saw no other option." My anger mounted, long buried under others' expectations. "But David, I don't really want to do that. Feels like another trap. I don't want to get near it."

"Well, then, what?" David egged me on.

"I'm not sure. What's seven weeks in Central City? Where I've seen people struggle with problems I never knew existed. I want to help but don't know where to begin. You know about my racism. Our neighbors pick it up fast."

"Sounds like you're workin' toward somethin'. What would you really like to do with your life?" Such a question—no one had ever asked me that before.

"I'm not sure. Something about working in neighborhoods like this." Putting down my sandwich, I looked at David. With her, I had found speech. "But the Society expects me to work in their schools, as a librarian. But I like being outdoors. Where real life happens. Around real people. What would you suggest?"

"You know Tulane's down the street from your convent on St. Charles Avenue," David said, screwing up her forehead. "They have a School of Social Work. Think a degree from there would ground you in your dream? With the courses and practicum, you might find out what you really want to do. Certainly, the Church needs trained helpers to serve the poor." She paused. "No one can forget what happened in our cities this summer. Riots and near riots spawned by decades of grindin' poverty and hot weather. Those poor people just blew their stacks. Created mayhem our government doesn't know how to handle. With some trainin', you might make a small difference in this mess."

"But that means I'd have to ask the Vicar for permission. We've a new one I've not met. I've never heard of anyone in the Society having a degree in social work. The Society's mission is education—to staff their academies and colleges."

"Well, Moloney, if you want to pursue your dream, you can at least ask. Perhaps even get permission to join me on weekends at St. Francis if you stay around here. I, too, have a dream—to open a multi-purpose center with free daycare, a methadone clinic, and thrift shop. Maybe after a few years, come work with me!"

"Perhaps you're right, David. At least I can ask."

And I did, and to everyone's surprise, Tulane awarded me a tuition waiver for my studies, beginning the following year. Until then, I was needed to teach English and religion classes at The Rosary. Even Reverend Mother Stanley's transfer at the end of that summer did not dampen my elation. Our impasse would continue. But I had David's support, together with memories of my play clothes, spurts of laughter, and fruity wines. More and more, the spent ruins of my thirty-two years were not such a disaster, especially in view of the renewal still to come to the Society.

Part 2

First Efforts to Dress Myself, 1967–1974

10

Black Flats with Square Toes, November 1967

And it did come, in November 1967, following the Special Chapter held at the motherhouse. Capitulants from our convents all over the world attended. Weeks of heated deliberation were sickened by the resignation of the Superior General, Reverend Mother Sabine DeValon. Until then, all Superior Generals had served in this capacity for life, as had the Society's foundress, St. Madeleine Sophie Barat.

While awaiting our new Vicar's visit to the Rosary, my "Sister dear" superior often cleared her throat and raised her shrill voice during evening recreations to regain control over her thirty-two nuns, seated in concentric circles in front of her in the community room. Few stitched or mended. The rule of silence and custody of the eyes were fast becoming relics of the past, like the modified habit. Some had already shortened them, styled the bangs peeking from beneath their veils, and tightened Velcro self-belts to enhance waistlines. I had done similarly. Older nuns pouted about the erosion of their lifestyle and complained loudly to Reverend Mother, not bothering to close the door to her office. Still heady with my summer's experiences in Central City, I could not imagine life in the Society without the Rule and Constitutions, largely unchanged from the time of their approbation by Pope Leo XII in 1826. But I itched for release from this austere life. The only quiet place in the convent was the chapel.

The November evening of Reverend Mother Mulqueen's arrival from St. Louis finally came. Change fever infected everyone who gathered around the pelican fountain in the circle drive to greet her. Bits of chatter floated on humid winds that presaged a storm. Standing on tiptoes, I scanned St. Charles Avenue for her. In her hands was our future in the Society.

Slowly, the station wagon pulled through the gates and stopped; from it emerged our new Vicar, a short stocky woman with a sallow complexion, plump jowls, clear-framed glasses on her squat nose; in her hand, a black satchel. Immediately, my "Sister dear" superior dropped to her knees to receive her blessing, then stooped to embrace her, amidst purring and cheers. It felt like kindergarten. Then, in turn, the Vicar greeted Reverend Mother's assistants and followed them to her office in the convent. This time, the door was closed.

With an hour before supper, I sat beneath a single bronze fixture in the chapel. Darkened stained-glass windows hemmed me in on all sides. Alone, on edge, I smoothed a fold in my habit and recalled Reverend Mother Melia's counsel, two years before at the motherhouse, about the changes coming to the Society. Tonight, I would learn of them, and with my vow of obedience, I must adjust. Questions about my future slammed me like birds trapped in a glass cage. Suddenly a spasm fired in my right knee.

Feverishly, I massaged it until hearing the bell for supper, then hurried to the refectory.

The Vicar stood next to my "Sister, dear" superior at the Mothers' table and led grace. With its "Amen," she smiled and shrugged her black veil over her shoulder, savoring our excitement.

"An historic evening for us all, Sisters!" she rasped in her New York accent. "Would you like to know one of the changes?" An eerie silence filled the refectory, as she continued, "The Superior General alone will be called Reverend Mother, and all the Vicars and local superiors will be called Mother." Giggles erupted; older nuns moaned. It was beginning. "So I'm Mother Mulqueen!" she added, "and to my right is Mother Stanley!" More raised eyebrows, sighs, commotion. Then with gusto, the Vicar rang the bell and said, "Since most are already talking, let's go all the way!"

From my place with the young professed in the back of the refectory, my plate of red beans and rice and mixed greens largely untouched, I continued scrutinizing the Vicar's lips for hints of what was to come. Her wide grin flashed toward her listeners, evoking still more merriment. Never had I seen them so animated, but I still couldn't pick up anything. With those around me, I'd just have to wait until recreation. Minutes dragged midst unnerving chatter. Too played out to speak, I forked the pecan pie especially baked for Mother Mulqueen on her first trip South.

Finally it was seven o'clock, the accustomed hour for recreation in the community room. Grabbing my sewing basket from the cupboard, I sat beneath blinking fixtures, studied the second hand sweeping the clock mounted next to the insurance calendar. Nasty winds rattled the shuttered windows, evoking whispers, giggles, rolling eyes among the younger nuns. Senior nuns were disgruntled by this charade and already threading their needles. The waiting continued.

Hurried footsteps in the corridor signaled the Vicar's approach. The sharp pleats in her skirts bespoke her disciplined life. Behind her glided Mother Stanley, wringing her hands, her pasty cheeks now like the swirls in peppermints. In her train followed her four assistants. Our buzzing lapsed into death-like silence, as we rose to greet them, watched them take their places in front of us, and sit down.

Mother Mulqueen's brown eyes darted behind rimless glasses and a grimace hardened her jaw as she flipped open her note-book, scrutinized the first page, and readied her pencil. Then she looked around the room. The hush deepened, needles poised in mid-air. My "Sister, dear" superior leaned against the back of her chair, her lips pursed. Lay sisters, stooped by years of manual work in the convent and grounds, sighed, their heads lowered over their mending. Older nuns scrutinized the tin-embossed ceiling, hoped for minimal changes in the Society; younger ones ached for its total revamping. I was somewhere in the middle.

In solemn tones, the Vicar began, her eyes glistening. "Good evening, Sisters! And it is good! Your weeks of prayer during the Special Chapter played a significant role. We felt a compelling presence among us, moving us beyond our agendas. The Spirit of Truth spoke through us. The renewal, mandated by the Sacred Congregation of the Affairs of Religious, was far greater than anyone could have envisaged. Its outcome amazed us." She paused, lowered her head, as if recalling the mood at the motherhouse. Then after wiping the tears welling in her eyes, she added, "Just as we've surrendered to these changes, we ask this of you."

My "Sister, dear" superior stared at the Vicar's blunt fingers tapping the pencil on the table in front of her, then seemed to be elsewhere. She knew what was coming. Outside, the St. Charles Avenue trolley clanged to a stop, then rumbled on.

Pulling herself from her reverie, Mother Mulqueen continued. "In obedience to our mandate, and after much deliberation, the Chapter Mothers voted to put aside our Rule and Constitutions for a period of experimentation. Dialogue and discernment with your superior will be the linchpins of this experimentation, based upon principles of Ignatian spirituality. Then we'll reconvene and formulate a new Rule and Constitutions to be approved by the Sacred Congregation." The Vicar's hand trembled as she checked off the first item in her notebook.

A gasp of disbelief rocked the room. I shuddered. That would mean engaging with my "Sister, dear" superior. At best, we tolerated each other. Never had we reviewed our impasse at Villa Duchesne. Other than her pressed habit and her chronic cough, I still had little sense of who she was. Suddenly, the proposed changes became bittersweet. I was not alone in my feelings. Older nuns squirmed on their cane-bottom chairs, and torn stockings slipped off their laps onto the floor. Too distraught to pick them up, they lowered their heads, folded their hands, and sighed. Another trolley rumbled by in the dark.

The Vicar noticed the troubled waters and paused until the turmoil lessened. Then in firm tones, she spelled out the implications of this renewal, beginning with our vows; they would remain in principle, but their practice would be experimental.

"Let's look at how this applies to our vow of poverty," she added. "Its intent, radical self-stripping in absolute trust upon the providence of God, remains the same. But in view of the expanding needs of your ministries to serve the people of God, its practice will differ. With the superior's permission, you'll have more items for your use. This is where dialogue comes in." I looked around. More bewilderment, long looks, sighs, anxiety, excitement—it felt as if we were being whirled in a centrifuge, powerless to flip off the switch.

I fidgeted with my silver ring, inscribed with my name and "Jesus et Marie," then recalled the celebrant's difficulty working it around my swollen knuckle during the Mass of Final Profession. It was still swollen. As a young professed in the Society, I had no idea what I'd need for my ministry. Never having one I could put my heart into, I had pretended to teach classes, because it was expected of me, so desperate I was for my superiors' approval. What the Vicar was describing sounded unattainable.

Next Mother Mulqueen addressed our vow of chastity; its intent would also remain in force—the renunciation of sexuality and generativity ever opening us to mystical marriage with God. But within the renewal, we were encouraged to develop friendships, both in the community and without, and thereby become more human. Our practice of custody of the eyes had precluded such intimacy, together with our rules of silence and cloister keeping us within the predictable Order of Day. Immediately I tingled, remembering the glow between one of nuns from last summer and her priest friend who had offered Mass around the coffee table in our wooded estate at Covington. I longed for something like that.

More excitement fired the community room. I blinked hard. The dismantling continued.

"And now for our vow of obedience," Mother added, her gaze sweeping over her sisters. "Its intent, to fashion our wills with

God's, articulated through our superiors, will remain." Here the Vicar's voice became firm. "Formerly, the superior, after prayer and conferring with her assistants, drew up ministries for her nuns based on the needs of the convent or school. However, with our new practice of the vow of obedience, this will change. Only through true dialogue between the superior and each nun can the will of God be discerned. Remember I've already described the primacy of dialogue and discernment in the renewal, tools we're called upon to practice."

Suddenly, I felt heartened. Evidently last summer's impassioned letter to her had made a difference. I would study at Tulane next year. Perhaps the new dialogue and discernment would work.

Across from me, older nuns shook their heads, distraught; younger ones grinned, anticipating still more change.

Then Mother Mulqueen paused, took a sip of water, fiddled with her pencil stub and notebook. Dark rains pelted the windows. There was still more. It was only seven-forty p.m.

Within the next twenty-five minutes, the Society's dismantling would be complete. No longer would the Order of Day marshal meditation, Office, Mass, examen, spiritual reading, one half hour of adoration, night prayers. Only daily Mass remained. We were now responsible for our own spiritual practices. I welcomed this change, easily distracted as I was by others in the chapel or community room.

Next discarded was the rule of silence. We could now speak, but in low tones, mindful of maintaining an atmosphere of prayer in the convent. This change perturbed me. I looked at those around me, many with flushed faces. Other than footfalls, coughs, and comments during shared recreation, I knew no one. I barely heard the Vicar add in thoughtful tones, "Nights, however, we'll still observe greater silence." (After retiring, no speaking until after Mass the next morning.)

Our torn stockings lay in heaps upon the floor. Outside, another trolley grated to a halt while a truck ground its gears and accelerated into the wet night.

And there was still more. The rule of cloister was dropped. We were free to move beyond the front gates, but not before signing the book kept in the portry by the front door, then signing in upon our return. Should we be out after hours, we were to take a house key. Even though I had tasted the excitement of Central City and Covington, I still feared the world around me, just as I had in St. Louis before entering Kenwood.

The Vicar lowered her head, checked that item off her list.

"And as for public and private penances with the Superior's permission," Mother said, "these are not in keeping with the renewal. So discontinue them." Much later I learned how such abuse created a pathological high that severed the body from spirit.

Then the Vicar paused, removed her glasses, cleaned them, adjusted them upon her wide nose, then scanned her notebook. "Just a few more changes," she added. "No longer will you only have newspaper clippings to keep you abreast of world events. Each morning the assistant will place *The Times-Picayune* on the reading table here in the community room." Catching Mother Stanley's eye, she added, "I understand there's an old television out in the shed, no longer used in the school library. We'll have it serviced and brought up here. We'll also get a radio and record player. Some records."

Suddenly, the world I'd left was getting uncomfortably close.

After checking off that item, Mother Mulqueen had still more to say, despite her voice becoming more gravelly. "The refectory will be renamed the dining room; it'll look different tomorrow. You'll see. And for feast days, we'll serve wine." Again I brightened. It would be like those weekends at Covington.

It was past eight o'clock.

"I've shared much with you this evening," Mother Mulqueen concluded, wrapping a rubber band around her notebook. "Allow the Holy Spirit to guide and strengthen your fidelity to the Society as we create a new way of living as daughters of St. Madeleine Sophie." She squinted as she stood and said, "I bid you good night and offer you God's blessing. I'll see you in the morning."

Disillusionment and giggles followed Mother and the others out of the community room. With my young professed persona in shambles around my worn shoes, I felt naked, strangely on my own with no Office, night prayers, or examen to end the day.

After Mass the next morning I followed others toward the dining room. Inside the door stood the grinning Vicar, morning puffiness banding her brown eyes.

Behind me, Mother Stanley regaled her listeners with a description of the refectory's transformation during the night. Tables and chairs, dragged over from the children's cafeteria, replaced the benches and oilcloth-covered tables. Absent also was the reader's chair, because we now spoke at all meals.

Savory aromas from somewhere in the back of the dining room excited my hunger. A new food warmer, I was told. I blinked hard beneath fluorescent fixtures enhancing the freshly polished floor, the contribution of the lay sisters. I mulled over still more changes: no bells to start or stop anything, no assigned places anywhere, no grace before or after meals, no rushed meals. My head spun.

I inched my way toward the food warmer, unnerved by shouts colliding against the twenty-foot ceiling. Standing on tiptoes, I spotted individually wrapped boxes of cereals lined upon racks. No more bowls of soggy Wheaties or Rice Krispies. Next to the platter of fresh fruit stood coffee urns replacing five-gallon pitchers formerly carted in from the kitchen. In front of me, some grumbled about the arrangement of the food, no longer placed in services for four on the tables. When my turn at the warmer finally came, I grabbed silverware from the basket, no longer pinned inside a napkin that was laundered each week. Then I filled my plate with scrambled eggs and sausages, grits, biscuits, and milk-gravy. Unable to locate cream for my coffee, I did without.

After seating myself with the young nuns, I looked around. At the end of the dining room, older ones slowly ate in silence, their eyes lowered. Not so at our table. Conversations thrummed around class schedules, gifted children, discipline problems, teaching methods, use of A/V equipment—one topic after another. These women, some of whom I'd known for years, bewildered me. Among them, I had no voice, just as I'd told David many times; similar to experiences with my family over meals. My uneasiness mounting, I watched for the earliest opportunity to absent myself.

"Well, Sisters, good morning to each of you! And it is good!" the Vicar said, stretching to her full height and clanking a spoon against her glass. "Today you begin adjusting to the changes." She waited for the din to subside.

"You like?" she quipped, panning the room. Not missing a beat, she took in the hooting and wide grins from younger nuns, sullen looks from older ones, their soiled dishes already stacked in front of them. "I thought you would. Many hands helped make this happen during the night. We'll take care of placemats and pictures later. Perhaps paint these dingy walls. Curtains for the windows." She paused, sipped her coffee, grimacing. "This is sure strong stuff! Chicory, you call it? No matter how much cream and sugar I add, it still bites me! Nothing like this in the East where I had my beginnings!" More titters flitted around the dining room like hesitant sparrows.

"I know many have to get over to the school," she said. "I'll be around for another day and together we can address some of your concerns." Looking toward the older nuns, her brown eyes tensed, she said, "Continue deepening your spiritual practices, now that you're on your own. Only within the quiet of prayer can we hear the guidance of the Holy Spirit. Our renewal depends upon deep listening. You have been faithful daughters of St. Madeleine Sophie, and I expect you'll continue to be!" Her comments quelled some of the uproar, but it resurfaced, as many took final gulps of coffee and rushed into their day.

While pushing myself out of my chair, I noticed my scuffed oxfords, the last pair packed in my steamer trunk for the Kenwood noviceship. They were beyond repair. I needed new ones. Having sighted Maison Blanche, the department store on Canal Street while driving with David last summer, I decided to ask my "Sister, dear" superior for permission for a new pair; they would become my Sunday shoes, the others for everyday use.

No words can describe my exhilaration fingering the convent charge card and riding the St. Charles Avenue trolley to Canal Street the following Saturday, and entering Maison Blanche.

Tentatively, I made my way toward women's shoes, already certain I would not buy another pair of oxfords. Displays of flats in black and blue and brown with square toes seized my attention; each sported a brass buckle, similar to shoes I'd worn before entering Kenwood. I picked up a black pair, carried them to an armchair, and hoped for a saleslady. Other patrons eyed my black habit, my stockinged feet. I waited, my glasses fogging with anticipation. I still remembered that blustery morning in Clark's, years before, shopping with Mother for my Kenwood trousseau. Then Mr. Pierce, the salesman, had squatted, as he fit me with brown and black oxfords, rubbers, and galoshes. I cringed noting the bulge between his meaty thighs.

Across from me, a blonde socialite said to a balding salesman, "I'll take those sandals, those pumps, and those boots. Charge them to my account. And hurry. I'm already late for my lunch date." It wouldn't be long before my turn came. Shoppers continued milling among tables of shoes on sale, occasionally picking up a pair, then seating themselves around me.

"And what can I do for you, Sister?" the same salesman asked.

It was just my luck. He'd have to do. "I'd like to try on these flats. Do you have them in my size? I usually wear an 8." I said, breathlessly. Mother was not with me this time. I was on my own.

His dark eyes puzzled, noting my oxfords with knotted laces, then at the black flats in my hands. "I'll see what I can find," he said, rushing back to the storeroom, perhaps suppressing an ill-timed question. While leaning back in my armchair, I studied mini-skirted women, preening in new footwear in front of floor mirrors; others, deep in thought, surveyed shoes spilling from boxes at their feet.

"Let's try on these," the salesman said, crouching on a stool in front of me. "If they don't work, we'll look for something else." His hands shook removing the flats from the box. First one, then the other he slipped onto my feet. Suddenly aware of my darned stockings, I blushed. I did have a newer pair. Then, I stood, walked around in a circle. These shoes would do, the forerunners of more changes to come.

"Really!" Mother gasped, her voice catching during our phone conversation a few days later. "That means you can come home for visits. I never thought that would happen. After ten years—I just don't know what to say." I imagined her toying with her pearls and sitting on the brocaded chair in the library at the top of the stairs.

"Yes, that's right," I said, doodling on the telephone directory in the darkened booth outside the superior's door. "We're free to leave the grounds, visit with friends and family. That sort of thing. Everyone's very excited." I did not breathe my ambivalence, so great was my need to still please her.

"Just let me know when you can come, and I'll freshen up your bedroom. It's been empty since Martha married. We'll also take care of your airfare."

After more family news, I thanked her and hung up, suddenly aware of multiple crosses I'd inked on the cover of the telephone directory. No longer was I the young professed described in my probation notes, and I knew it. Sucked into the euphoria of the renewing Church, I was strangely energized. Yet emptiness still clamored for clues as to who I was. As in my family of origin, I became invisible, voiceless during meals with the nuns. Yet I had my new Sunday shoes, a harbinger of more changes.

11

Green Plaid Shirtwaist Dress, November 1968

A painful year followed, the experimentation firestorming through the community. Corridors buzzed with prolonged conversations. Some became ill and spent time in the infirmary. Unable to mediate this turmoil, my "Sister, dear" superior outfitted a separate room for the younger nuns' recreation, an effort to assuage the distress among the older ones; it only widened the split between us.

In November 1968, the week before my thirty-third birthday, I again boarded the trolley for Canal Street and The Tall Shop I'd spotted during other trips downtown, the convent charge again card in my pocket. Another impassioned letter to Mother Mulqueen had resulted in permission to wear secular clothes on the Tulane campus where I was now studying. Thus attired, I hoped to become more relevant to the professors and classmates, among whom I still felt isolated. But there were stipulations: my dress hems had to fall below my knees, no matter that mini-skirts were the rage. And upon returning home from Tulane, I was to put on the habit for the remainder of the day.

Outside grimy windows of the trolley, blocks clattered by, as questions tested my resolve. Would secular clothes make a difference on the Tulane campus? What about my weight gain? Would anything fit? I used to wear size 14 or 16, but that was ten years ago. Passing motorists had no idea what a momentous morning this was for me. Finally we approached my stop and I yanked the cord, then eased myself down the steps of the trolley onto the street, my other hand catching my veil flapping in the wet breeze.

Ahead of me was The Tall Shop, its display windows filled with mannequins dressed in turtleneck sweaters, fringed vests, bell-bottom slacks, and A-line dresses, styles I longed to wear, like my classmates'. Passersby stared as I pulled open the door, the interior heady with smells of fresh merchandise.

A saleslady smartly dressed in beige tones and gold jewelry observed my habit and in faltering tones, drawled, "My name is Sophie. How may I help you?" An embarrassed silence fell between us until I found words.

"Thanks," I said, again fingering the convent charge card in my pocket. "I can use some help. I'm looking for a couple of outfits for the Tulane campus where I'm studying." To my right, racks of colorful dresses drew my gaze.

"Well, I declare! This is a first for me!" she exclaimed, her cheeks blushing. "Comin' out of the habit? I didn't know that could be done!" Her enthusiasm drew her co-workers, also eyeing my habit.

"Aren't you a Madame of the Sacred Heart?" another asked, her face brightening. I nodded. "My sister's children went to The

Rosary. She always spoke highly of the Madames' distinctive habits—unlike those worn by other communities in our city." I smiled, knowing she was right. "But how come you want to get out of it? Wear dresses and things like that?"

My words about becoming more relevant to people jammed on themselves like Velcro. Nothing made sense to my questioner, who was clearly rattled by my decision.

"Well, let's see now!" Sophie said, stepping forward, her wits returning. She adjusted her glasses upon her pointed nose, scrutinized my size, and added, "You'll probably need a slip for starters. Follow me over to the racks and let's see what appeals to you." Another shopper gawked, the scarves she was examining limp in her hands. Sophie continued, "Shouldn't be hard to find something for you to wear at Tulane. Let's look! Probably a size 12 or 14?" I nodded. She flipped through dresses, skirts, blouses, presenting their styles, fabrics and color for my inspection, then piled likely selections over her arm. "Follow me to the dressing room, Sister, and let's see what works!"

Alone before the mirror surrounded by colorful outfits hanging on hooks, I stared at the image of this habited nun on the brink of serious change, then looked hard from several angles. Was there a woman beneath this blackness? I had come a long way from those weekend jaunts, two summers ago, when I wore that red shirt and plaid shorts and sandals. Still studying my reflection, I removed my celluloid headband and veil, ran fingers through my matted hair, still brunette and thick. Then I unfastened the Velcro tabs on my habit and pulled off the bulky cotton slip. Another look in the mirror. This time, my soiled bra cupped button breasts.

"Are you decent?" Sophie asked, pushing some slips through the curtains. "I guessed one of these would fit. Let me know if they don't." Her voice had heartened me, and I wiggled into the slip with lace trim; its silkiness tantalizing. Again, I looked into the mirror and marveled at my ivory shoulders. Only in my hand mirror, included in my trousseau for the noviceship, had I glimpsed parts of me, because larger mirrors were considered worldly.

Another look in the mirror revealed an empty stool in the corner of the dressing room. My mother wasn't here to scrutinize my outfits. I was on my own. My fingers trembled unbuttoning, unzipping dresses, blouses, and jackets. All size 12s worked, one more attractive than another. Time had stopped.

"May I take a look?" Sophie asked from outside the curtains. I had just fastened the belt of a green plaid shirtwaist dress and was admiring my reflection.

"Yes," I exclaimed, parting the curtain, stepping backwards.

"Sister, you look gorgeous, if you don't mind my saying so! Come out into the store and walk around. Get a feel for your new look."

I did as she advised, catching reflections of myself in the eyes of patrons and salesladies.

Dazed, I returned to the dressing room, gripped my shoulders, and made a face in the mirror. I wanted to buy everything I'd tried on, but that was absurd. Like my own mother, my "Sister, dear" superior would probably have me return most of what I would bring home. I must decide. The plaid shirtwaist dress with long sleeves, for sure. Again, I tried on the mock leather jumper with the crimson turtleneck sweater; then the blue A-line dress for special occasions. Yes, these would do. Suddenly, a confident woman grinned and looked back at me. I had made a significant beginning.

Elizabeth

That night after supper, my "Sister, dear" superior insisted I model my new outfits for the younger nuns seated on the floor in her office, their black skirts hiked above their calves. The doors were closed, the shades drawn. Curious eyes scrutinized my shapely body, alternately attired in vibrant greens, reds and browns, and soft blues. Questions rained upon me: where I had shopped, the cost of each outfit, the styles, fabrics, colors, etc. Even the new slip, at no cost, Sophie had included with my outfits. Dry-mouthed, I heard my wispy voice responding. For the first time my peers saw me. My moment in the sun was blinding.

Then it was over. "Sister, dear," Mother interjected, "we better wind this up. It's getting late. We still observe greater silence, you know." Her feverish eyes betrayed her desire to wear secular clothes. Everyone ached to do likewise, and soon.

The following Monday, wearing my shirtwaist dress, I sat in a drafty conference hall for my class in Social Process, balancing notebooks on my lap. I felt conspicuous, my swollen knees no longer covered by the skirts of my habit. I drew my black flats beneath me, felt my calves chilled by musty rains. Would anyone comment on my new dress, my brunette hair that feathered my oval face? A later stop at Maison Blanche's beauty salon had worked wonders with my matted hair.

I checked my watch. Professor Zimmerman was late. More classmates slouched into the hall, rubbing sleep from their eyes, balancing coffee mugs with book bags. Others coughed, chatted, meandered to their chairs. I felt strangely alone. Only an Ursuline nun in her black habit gave me a curious look, one I quickly dismissed. Her community was not as far into the Vatican renewal as ours was.

Yet I had made a beginning.

Green Plaid Shirtwaist Dress, November 1968

My mother's curiosity mounted with these changes I conveyed in weekly letters. As my need for a secular wardrobe grew, she responded quickly. A yellow cardigan soon complemented my shirtwaist dress, then a black leather shoulder-strap bag. Rather than ask my "Sister, dear" superior's permission to use them, I tucked them in my drawer. Violating my vow of poverty did not seem to matter. The young nuns did notice my varied wardrobe but said nothing; their cool regard said it all. But I was not perturbed. Mother was happy to provide for my needs, in a way that was unlike my childhood. Besides, I was learning how to become a social worker. My identity enlarged each morning I set foot outside the convent gates, despite knee pain and exhaustion.

Cotton Checkered Suit,
August 1970

Mother's letters also applauded my progress through Tulane School of Social Work: the completion of my course work and practicums at Kingsley House and the Algiers Mental Health Clinic. During weekend visits to New Orleans, she treated me to more outfits at The Tall Shop: an all-weather coat for St. Louis winters and tailored dresses that filled my chifferobe. Her tastes had become mine. Among hundreds of classmates the morning of my January graduation, I stool tall in a tangerine matching dress and coat, textured with swirling lines. Graduating with honors elated me and drew David's congratulations; she was standing next to my parents. My "Sister, dear" superior was also in the audience with two other nuns from my community.

That afternoon I was admitted to Touro Infirmary for my first set of knee surgeries—synovectomies, Dr. Saer called them, to relieve intractable pain. In my suitcase was a new bathrobe from Mother, since I didn't have one. Afterwards, leering incisions on my knees seemed to ape months of physical therapy, drugs, and insomnia. Twenty-five-pounds lighter, I learned to walk again.

Almost independent of my cane by the summer, I reviewed the responses I'd received from social-work administrators to whom I'd mailed my resume. On a hunch, I telephoned Associated Catholic Charities in downtown New Orleans and was invited to interview for a caseworker position the next day. Not having anything appropriate to wear, or so I believed, I remembered David's thrift shop, Bethlehem House of Bread, recently opened near Central City. With the right outfit, I would assuredly impress my employers and win the position. I had no other options. Mother and her checkbook were in St. Louis.

It was a steamy afternoon in June when I pulled open the door of David's place, stepped inside the paneled office, and rang the bell. Within minutes, heavy footfalls sounded. It was David, a coverall over her white habit.

"Moloney, what brings you here?" David asked, eyeing my cotton shift and flats, my cane hitched to the edge of the counter. She still decried my secular clothes. "Play clothes within the privacy of the convent is one thing, but on the streets, how'll anyone know you're a nun?" she had often said. I had no response, so wedded was I to discovering who I was. Somehow secular clothes helped.

After I explained my needs to David, she led me to her thrift shop, adjacent to her free daycare center and methadone clinic for poor women, then shuffled off to the kitchen. Alone in this dank room with poor lighting, I rooted through racks of clothing for the perfect suit, the perfect blouse to accompany it. Unable to stand much longer, I spotted a checkered cotton suit and taupe jewelneck blouse, both size 12s, and held them up to myself. A soft voice said, "These will do, nicely!"

Strangely, David grinned as she bagged my outfit, handed it to me, free of charge, then wished me well for tomorrow's interview.

I did get that position, providing casework services to juvenile girls the courts placed at Our Lady of the River School in Bridge City, Louisiana, a facility staffed by cloistered Good Shepherd Sisters. Their rule precluded social workers. That was where I fit in. To fulfill my responsibilities, my community purchased a 1959 VW for my use during the week. How I obtained my driver's license would take us too far afield.

During my third week on the job, Sister Christina, one of the housemothers, phoned, her voice frantic. Earlier that morning, thirteen-year-old Ruthie's bed had been empty when she went to waken her and the others in the dormitory. She had made it across the fields, climbed the fence, and was gone. I was to follow up with the juvenile authorities and keep Sister informed, because she wanted Ruthie back.

I panicked, grabbed Ruthie's chart bulging with court summaries of deviant behaviors, and headed for Valerie Bernadas, my supervisor. She already knew Ruthie had refused to see me in the visitors' center, and that I was taken by her story: motherless at four years of age, an alcoholic father more interested in his next drink, several failed foster-home placements.

"Close the door, Sister, and sit down," said Valerie, a matronly woman in an A-line dress, her glasses resting upon her chest. "I've already heard about Ruthie. Sergeant Phillips just phoned. She's made it to her father's house in the French Quarter!" A smile glimmered in her blue eyes, recessed within plump cheeks lightly made up. "This'll be a good learnin' experience for you. Just do what I say. After a while, you'll get the knack of handlin' such cases. Although I admit they still suck the wind out of me after all these years!"

I breathed easier, sitting across from Valerie. Silvering hair feathered her square face, softening it.

"The first thing we have to do, Sister, is check on Ruthie," she said, fiddling bead bracelets on her suntanned wrist. "Having been in detention so many times, her probation officer's allowing her to remain with her father until the hearing—an unsavory character, that one! Nasty over the phone! Refused to let me interview him when I worked on Ruthie's placement for the sisters." Between Valerie's eyes ran fault lines of annoyance, suggesting years of broaching parental resistance. Quickly lowering her gaze, she concluded, "Let me know what you come up with when you get back. Then we'll talk about the psychosocial summary for the court."

With Ruthie's home address stuck to my steering wheel, I snaked through narrow streets in the French Quarter. Lots littered with refuse and tangled with impenetrable chicory and thistles surrounded boarded-up shotgun houses. In one yard a tomcat lurked under a sagging lawn chair. No other signs of life. Again, I checked the address. The right street, but where was the house? My misgivings mounted. I had earlier found the father's phone number disconnected.

I pulled over to the curb, and, with my cane, began walking. The morning sun fired my back as I searched for the right house. I almost passed one with bleached numbers above its mailbox. That could be it. I pulled open the gate that flailed on a broken hinge, approached the front stoop, and rang the bell. No answer. Then I rapped on the door, splotched with soot. A long pause. I jumped. The tomcat darted under a derelict pickup truck stripped of its wheels. Perceiving no one home, or willing to answer the door, I turned to leave, but the door scraped open. Upon the sagging threshold stood a squat pot-bellied man in faded cut-offs, the remains of breakfast on his T-shirt; next to him, a forlorn teenager with scraggly blonde hair, her hand draped around his waist.

"What ye doin' 'round here?" he snarled. "I'se no time for company! I got bisness to 'tend to!" His unshaven jowls hardened, his sodden body listed to the right, as he placed his hand on the girl's sunburned shoulders. Bird-like, she gazed at me, her china blue eyes flickering. Chigger bites covered her arms and legs, skinned and bruised from the morning's run.

"I'm Sister Moloney, caseworker with Catholic Charities," I faltered, sickened by the stench from the darkened interior. "I'm looking for Ruthie and her dad. I was led to believe they lived on this street. Might you be Ruthie from Our Lady of the River School? I never had the chance to meet you." She shrugged, moved closer to her father, one bare foot cradled atop the other.

"Git! Git out of here! Ruthie's stayin' right here by me! That place ye run is a dump! She told me all 'bout it! Never will she go back there! She's my daughter! I'se the right to say where she lives! Now git off my property! Git! Git!" His slanted eyes exploded in rage. Ruthie darted behind her father, her stained fingers clinging to his bronze belt buckle.

I returned to the office, turning the wrong way down one-way streets, drawing blasts and catcalls from other motorists, my street map opened on my lap. Behind me, a laundry truck rode my bumper, and I swerved to the side of the road and stopped, then leaned my forehead upon the steering wheel, hot and played out. More honking. It was a police car. I was illegally parked.

"Did you get in, Sister? Did you see Ruthie?" Valerie asked, polishing her bifocals. I nodded, crestfallen. Not missing a beat, she added, "See what I meant 'bout troubled familes referred to us by the court? No matter!" She stretched her back into her chair and said, "What impressions did you pick up? You know, home visits are our primary diagnostic tool." To my surprise, the few moments on that front stoop expanded into a ten-minute narrative. Valerie leaned forward, savoring every word. "Good for you, Sister! You picked up more than enough information to nail Ruthie's father. I'm certain the judge will rule in our favor. Now pull together a psychosocial summary. Frances will type it for you and deliver it to the court."

Before the end of the day, Valerie called me, "Ruthie's hearing is scheduled for Friday, downtown in the Juvenile Courts. Her father's hired a lawyer to plead his case. You'll represent Our Lady of the River School." Pausing, she asked, "Are you still with me? A lot to handle, I know, but you'll get through it—stop by before you go home and we'll review the protocol for such hearings."

Friday morning, wanting to impress the judge with my aplomb, I wore my jewelneck blouse and cotton checkered suit. With a copy of Ruthie's psychosocial summary in my notebook, I headed downtown for the hearing. After pushing through the revolving doors of the Juvenile Courts building, flanked by pots of flaming hibiscus, I strode into the marble foyer, teeming with policemen, court officials, anxious parents. After obtaining directions to Judge O'Connor's chambers, I stopped at a drinking fountain, my thoughts all ajumble. If only Valerie could have come with me, shown me how to conduct myself during such hearings. Yet she trusted me enough to do this on my own. Then I remembered David's counsel: "No one knows what's really best for Ruthie. Step back, Liz. It'll work itself out. There's a wisdom here, far greater than anyone can discern, let alone this judge, known for his deals."

After getting off the elevator, I spotted Ruthie and her father sitting on a bench outside the judge's chambers. From an overhead window, sunlight spilt upon her curly hair, shampooed for this occasion, a hesitant smile upon pale lips. Looking like a moppet in a striped sundress and flats, she folded her hands in her lap, demurely pressing her knees together. Her father, sporting a clean shirt and jeans, looked away when I approached. "Ruthie, I'm glad to see you!" I called out, excitedly. Mistrust hazed her blue eyes, and she leaned against her father.

I hurried inside the judge's chambers and took a seat behind one of two tables, arranged in front of a mahogany desk flanked by American and Louisiana flags. At the other table was Ruthie's lawyer, absently drumming on his briefcase, his tie askance across his bowl-shaped chest. A tan-uniformed sheriff looked bored, fidgeting with handcuffs snapped to his wide belt. The judge was already twenty-five minutes late. Quietly, I reviewed the points from my summary I planned to make when called upon by the judge.

Suddenly, the door behind the desk opened, and the sheriff announced Judge O'Connor, a short balding man, the vest of his three-piece suit pinching his abdomen. Winking at the lawyer, he tossed a thick file upon his desk, jammed a cigar into his mouth, and eased himself onto a swivel chair. Then he rasped, "We're here to talk about Ruthie, who's back again. And what's in her best interests, now." He raised bushy eyebrows. "We've reviewed her record, listened to counsel her father engaged for this hearing, and decided Ruthie should return to him. Case closed!" I wanted to protest but had no voice. The lawyer across from me smirked. I remained in my chair as the room emptied. Evidently looking sharp in my new suit did not matter.

Sister Christina was not happy with the outcome, nor was Valerie, but she understood the system. She'd been burnt as well.

Later Ruthie's story was lost within school talk over supper in our dining room. Still voiceless among the nuns, I looked for the first opportunity to absent myself and call David. Later, my checkered suit and blouse remained stuffed in the back of my chifferobe.

13

Cotton Nightgown, March 1974

Multiple stresses led to further breakdown of my body: the virulent spread of rheumatoid arthritis destroying the new synovial lining in my knees, ineffective pain medications, constipation and exhaustion, frustrating casework with juvenile girls, my shadow existence among the nuns I lived with. The only respites from this insanity were fleeting highs after the second or third glass of wine during happy hours among the nuns, Saturday evenings, in elegant homes of the superior's friends—more experiments in community living. My need for attention grew like a cancer. I was floundering. My mother knew nothing of these stresses, or so I thought.

Finally in 1972 a new superior, Margaret Fraser, noted my emotional difficulties and recommended a psychiatrist, Dr. Francis Kane. If not him, then another might be able to help me. Initially I balked but later knew she was right and telephoned his receptionist for an appointment at his office in DePaul Hospital.

Fingering the tie of my wrap-around skirt, I limped into Dr. Kane's waiting room, its walls lined with framed credentials and watercolors of sky-blue fields. In front of them worked a receptionist, her ringed fingers attacking the keys of an electric typewriter. She nodded, as I lowered myself onto an armchair, placed my cane next to my pumps. Dry-mouthed, I waited, gripping my hands in my lap.

Then the inner office door flew open. I looked up. A teenager with stringy hair, swollen eyes, and beads jangling upon her chest rushed past me, moaning. Behind her stood the psychiatrist with curly grey hair, ruddy cheeks, intense blue eyes, and a starched medical coat over his robust frame. I blinked hard.

"Sister Moloney?" he smiled. "I'm Dr. Kane. Come into my office." His clipped speech suggested New England origins. Fumbling for my cane, I followed, my heels catching on the thick carpet. On his desk sat a bronze ashtray with a pipe, still fragrant. Next to it, a new chart, conceivably mine, and next to it, the latest issue of *Commonweal*, a liberal Catholic monthly. His clean-shaven jaw softened as he said, "Your superior thought I might be of help to you."

I froze. How much of my story had she shared with him— my sullen looks, my demands to be heard during meals, my expanding wardrobe, my strange love affair with wine? That one evening Mother Fraser and I met on the convent's verandah still spooked me. Recently arrived from our school in Taiwan, she appeared youthful in her cotton dress and sandals. Soft breezes tickled loose strands of wavy hair upon her tanned forehead. She was a different kind of mother who intuited the brokenness I denied and sought a remedy.

Our hour began. Cradling his pipe in blunt fingers, Dr. Kane invited me to speak of anything. For what seemed like forever, I blurted out pieces of my life, nothing connecting with anything else. I was lost in my words and knew it. Yet he listened.

"Very good, Sister," Dr. Kane finally interjected. "Let me tell you something about my training as a Freudian analyst. Perhaps you're familiar with this orientation?" I nodded, having covered it during my Tulane classes. "Good. Then I suggest we meet five more times. See how we work together. If analysis seems appropriate, we'll go ahead with it. If not, perhaps you can see another psychiatrist." I nodded, his comments echoing as if from a distant land. Then he added, "Next time, let's talk about your family."

"Dr. Kane, I've prepared this social summary of my family for your review," I said the following week, as I handed it to him. After crossing my sandaled feet, I begin reading from my copy: names, relationships, births, places, my voice rough-riding over the facts. No faltering as during our last hour. Dr. Kane looked puzzled over his tortoise-shell glasses, his eyes listless. I stopped, my discomfort extreme.

"Sister, why don't you just tell me about your family. I can read about them myself." Reaching for his pipe, he scraped its bowl with a pick, tapped spent grains into an ashtray.

"Shall I start all over?" I mumbled.

"Yes, please."

I began again, my words even more disconnected than last week. Silences yawned between impressions of my parents, my siblings. Only thirty minutes had passed. I shifted in my chair, recrossing my feet. Suddenly, I made a sickening discovery: I didn't know my family, despite having grown up among them.

"Thank you, Sister Moloney. That will be all for today. Next week, let's talk about the nuns you live with." He stood, smoothing his maroon tie under his medical coat, his blue eyes steely with concern. No smile this time.

Starts and stops filled the following hours with Dr. Kane: sketches of nuns I lived with, my co-workers at Catholic Charities, my clients. More truth emerged: my fragile identities as a professed member in the Society of the Sacred Heart and a child-welfare worker. No organized sense of self had ever developed. As long as I could remember, I had been hell-bent on meeting others' expectations; their approval alone gave meaning to my life. Nevertheless, I slowly warmed towards Dr. Kane, who held the shards of my thirty-seven years in his strong hands, and I agreed to analysis, four times each week. Rather than medicate my depression, he believed I could talk my way through.

So we began.

Painful months followed. Lying on Dr. Kane's couch in his shadowy office, I heard my voice for the first time in my life. Albeit wispy, it spoke truth. I did not like it, but I knew not to miss a single appointment with myself, after the process was underway. Besides, Dr. Kane was listening, occasionally jotting notes on his pad, another new experience for me. At length, a disturbing pattern began to emerge: my isolation from people, places, and things. Even God had abandoned me in the aftermath of my knee surgeries. For years, I had sensed there was little substance within me, but now I experienced its appalling emptiness and wept. No longer could I pretend behind smiles that soured. I had no reason to smile.

More and more, I depended upon Dr. Kane's listening presence. We were engaged in deep-sea mining to salvage the lost pieces of myself. Tethered to Dr. Kane's energy, I entered into a limbo world and waited to hear what I would say next. And the revelations continued, especially dreams that imprinted themselves upon my waking moments. One kept recurring.

I am wearing the Society's long black habit, fluted cap, and veil, their shabbiness bespeaking years of neglect, my tarnished profession cross askew upon my sunken chest. I sit inside a dingy factory filled with noisy conveyor belts spewing cylinders. At their terminus stand black-garbed nuns, feverishly boxing and tabulating them, lest they fail to meet the manager's expectations. Productivity is everything as noted on faded placards lining the walls. Bewildered, I watch, anxious to participate but not knowing how. Nothing makes sense.

Other dreams with similar themes hounded me. Still powerless to effect change in my outer world, I explored them within Dr. Kane's presence, then promptly forgot them until jarred by another.

Months of free association emptied into another year of analysis, a process hidden from my mother. I was beginning to see her dominance over me but was still too weak to confront her.

Then in March 1974, I started up in bed, blinking furiously, my head splitting, my pillow saturated with perspiration, my cotton nightgown balled around my thighs. It was one-thirty. A numinous dream commanded my full attention.

It is night. I am preparing to go out. I put on my winter coat, reach for my gloves, then force the right-handed one onto my left hand. It won't work. I am furious. I tug harder, scream.

I crawled out of bed toward the bathroom, flipped on the light, stripped, tossed aside my cotton nightgown with the cache number 64 stitched on the front, worn since the noviceship, then towel-dried my body before the mirror. My brown eyes, hooded with grief, terrified me. I turned away, then put on the frilly gown Mother had given me for Christmas. After returning to bed, sleep did not come. Fitfully, I watched the hours pass until dawn. Already, I intuited the dream's meaning.

Later that afternoon lying on Dr. Kane's couch, I sandwiched the numinous dream between work-related issues, then shut down. A long silence followed. I repositioned my aching knees, while studying the meandering crack in the ceiling, the webbed pattern the small lamp behind me threw upon the wall, habits I often resorted to when bereft of words. Suddenly I heard myself dredging up the dream, then stormed, "I can't do it anymore! It won't work! I've got to get out of the Society! Take a leave of absence for starters, like others have done!" More silence followed until another painful memory pressed itself upon me. I would speak.

"Dr. Kane, I'm back in the community room at Villa Duchesne… evening recreation… It's January 1967… The whole community is there, including my 'Sister, dear' superior. I'm extremely stressed. I yell, 'I feel like I'm stifling in a narrow box. It's nailed shut! I've got to get out!' No one says anything, and after an interval, one of the nuns picks up the accustomed banter with the superior." I began sobbing. Dr. Kane placed the Kleenex within reach. More silence completed the hour.

Still wiping my eyes as I left Dr. Kane's office, I noted his curious smile, and even more curious words. "It's about time, Sister! See you tomorrow." This was one of the few times he spoke during our analysis, lest he influence this decision I had to make on my own. But it still had to be implemented. I knew many would be disappointed, and they were. Nevertheless, I found voice enough with the Vicar who granted me a six-month leave of absence from the Society.

The weekend before my move into a furnished two-bedroom apartment recommended by a co-worker at Catholic Charities, I flew to St. Louis, my parents again covering the expense. On the way to their home, we stopped at Glen Echo Country Club for supper. Rather than tell them my plans over the phone, I wanted to tell them in person.

Inside The Grille, I noted dad's sports jacket draping his shoulders, his sparse hair, his chronic cough. Still he lit up a cigarette and inhaled deeply, all the while looking at me. Mother, too, appeared thinner in her St. John's knit suit, with more worry lines creasing her forehead, more grey in her tightly curled hair. Their concern for me stung. Other members in The Grille, drinks in hand, still in golf attire, listened to a newsreader analyze Cannonade's 2:04 run at the Kentucky Derby earlier that afternoon.

After the waiter brought our drinks, then took our orders, I began, hoping my chardonnay would loosen my tongue. "For a long time, I've been unhappy in the Society. I tried to hold on. I thought our renewal would change things, but it only worsened them. I've been given a leave of absence to sort things out. I'll be moving next Saturday." With this disclosure, I breathed easier, gulped more wine and waited. I made no mention of the numinous dream or my analysis with Dr. Kane during the past two years.

Mother's blue eyes suddenly lost their hardness, as she reached for my hand and said, "Liz, I'm not surprised. I've always known you were unhappy, but I never wanted to pry—those surgeries and learning to walk, learning to use your right hand. So much pain. I ached for you. Besides, I don't know how you stood it all those years, living with those women—women are so hard to get along with. I never could have done what you did." Her warmth startled me. Never had she spoken like that. In disbelief, I took another swallow of wine, then slipped off my profession ring and thrust it in my pocket.

Dad was silent. His brown eyes misted as he inhaled his cigarette, coughed again, and swallowed more scotch. Then he said, sadly, "Liz, you'll let me know if you need financial help."

"Tell us about your apartment," Mother said, brightening. "Where is it? What do you need to set up housekeeping?" In such matters, she was still the expert. My face dropped. I needed everything. The convent had provided only the down payment and first month's rent on the furnished apartment, a saucepan with a lid, a few odd dishes, a sugar bowl, and a handful of Green Stamps, together with the VW for my work. Whatever else I needed would come from the salary I was given to use during my leave of absence, except for Dr. Kane's charges. Those the Society would continue picking up.

"Well, before your flight tomorrow, we'll go shopping. Get whatever you need," Mother said, her voice hardening with control. My previous resolve to outfit my apartment from my biweekly paycheck frittered away in view of her offer. Despite yearning for independence, I buckled under her power. With the second glass of chardonnay, it did not seem to matter.

And we did shop, lavishly, at Famous-Barr.

While waiting for the arrival of my stash, I used the pink towel I had swiped from the superior's bathroom the morning I left the convent, made do with stained pillows and spreads, scooped up dust balls and insects from the threadbare carpet. The structure of my work week, the few friends I'd made in the office, my next-door neighbors, Marge and Frank Silver, both former religious who had met on the Notre Dame campus, afforded me ballast as I began life anew.

Despite continuing depression and chronic fatigue, despite arthritic knee pain, five months later I did leave the Society after signing papers sent from the Sacred Congregation for Religious and Secular Affairs, renamed by Pope Paul VI in 1967. I was thirty-nine years old. Yet I still wore that cotton gown with the cache number 64 stitched on the front.

Part 3

Regression,
1974–1987

14

White Spring Coat,
May 1976

Thrust from the security of my "other mother" in the Society of the Sacred Heart, I was all the more thrown upon my own mother and her weekly letters and gifts and occasional phone calls. My neediness escalated with her attention, despite what I heard myself say during analysis with Dr. Kane. My self-understanding still undefined, I held on to both helpers. Thus I continued maintaining my apartment, showing up for work each morning, entertaining co-workers, and exercising at The First Lady three evenings each week upon the recommendation of my doctor. Sunday morning Mass with my neighbors, the Silvers, continued. Through a new friend, an ex-Carmelite nun, I began attending singles parties, juiced by alcohol and cigarettes and jarring music, but was rarely asked to dance. Much of this, however, was only filling up time. I remained lonely, often lost. I had the body of a woman, I dressed like one—even had my ears pierced—but had no sense of who breathed inside, half-sick as I was with arthritic pain. So the year passed.

Holidays, my parents continued mailing me round-trip tickets to St. Louis to their spacious home in the Hanley Tower Condominium, affording me a longer respite. However Dad's debilitation, described in Mother's letters—hypertension, weight loss, dizziness, knee pain, and frequent nosebleeds requiring trips to St. Mary's emergency room—gave me pause. He had been mailing monthly checks to cover Dr. Kane's expenses. It never occurred to me to cut back my visits and budget them within my salary. Finally in March 1976, Dad's doctor confirmed a diagnosis of oat cell lung cancer and admitted him to St. Mary's Hospital for chemotherapy.

During the following months, Mother's phone calls kept me abreast of his treatment, complicated by multiple infections, strokes, and congestive heart failure, necessitating treatment in ICUs. Daily at his bedside, she endured each crisis supported by my siblings and their families. My alarm deepened. I was not with them.

Easter weekend, I flew to St. Louis and joined Mother at Dad's bedside. Skeletal, sallow in a faded gown, he lay motionless, a feeding tube in his nose, a central line in his neck, his hands laced in leather mittens and tied to the raised bedrails, a catheter bag with discolored urine hanging on the bed frame. Hours passed, punctuated by the wheezing ventilator. Only when the nurse came to feed him did he open his eyes, those same eyes that used to pine for me, those same discomfiting eyes that led me to seek Mother's protection, although I never knew why.

Suddenly, Dad stirred, his brown eyes glowing as he turned his head and whispered, "How beautiful you are, Liz! Yes! So beautiful! Beautiful!" Never had he spoken to me like that. Each word became a spinning sun illuminating the impasse that had existed between us since that hot summer night on the sleeping porch when I was six years old. Stunned, I clenched my hands, lowered my eyes. Then he said to Mother, "How beautiful she is, isn't she?" Then he closed his eyes.

Mother squirmed in her chair, nodded, and let it go at that. We never spoke of this experience. Still needing her support, I could not afford to.

The morning after my return to New Orleans, I had this troubling dream:

My phone rings. It is the hospital calling to inform me that Dad is dying. I should come quickly. Upon my arrival, I learn Dad has already died, his remains placed on a gurney in the corridor outside the morgue. As I approach the sheet-draped form, Dad's penis becomes erect.

Dr. Kane offered no elucidation of this dream when next we met. I did not ask for one.

Finally the phone call came on May 16, 1976. A third cardiac arrest ended Dad's sixty-nine years of life while still in St. Mary's Hospital. A nurse had been working with him when he breathed his last.

A somber mood filled Mother's family room when I arrived later that afternoon. She and my brothers had just returned from making funeral arrangements at Kriegshauser's.

"It hurts! Right here!" Mother blurted, balling her fist over her heart. "And we were preparing to bring my darling home with home care this coming week—the maintenance men knew to remove his bed to make room for the hospital bed I'd ordered. I wanted him close to me." Grief had sunk her ashen face, hollowed her blue eyes, puffy and inflamed, and wasted her body.

Instantly, my world collapsed within hers. After acknowledging my presence, Mother snatched a handkerchief from the pocket of her wool suit dress and retired to her bedroom. I was speechless, despite being versed in Elizabeth Kübler-Ross's material on death and its effects upon the survivors, a study I felt compelled to make because of Dad's terminal diagnosis.

While stashing my suitcase in the hall closet, I suddenly felt like a stranger among my siblings with nothing to do except wait for tomorrow's wake and funeral the following morning. They had made all the decisions. No one needed my help, nor did I know how to offer it. As in my childhood, I was voiceless, fading in and out while listening to them, drinks and cigarettes in hand. When a lull occurred, I asked about Mark, our youngest brother, sixteen years my junior, who was studying for a degree in art history at the Villa Schifanoia in Florence, Italy.

"We called him," John said, swishing an ice cube in his drink. "Because he's in the midst of finals, he decided not to come for the funeral." Other topics flew into the maelstrom, and so it went for the remainder of the afternoon.

I missed Mark. I still remembered his unexpected visit before I had left the convent in May 1974. Before then, I had had little contact with him.

"Hello, Liz," he had said, extending his arms in welcome as I approached him in the front parlor, its tall windows opened to morning breezes.

"This is such a surprise, Mark," I said, noting his smile. "What brings you to New Orleans?"

"I've always wanted to return here, on my own. You may remember I came to see you with Mother and Dad when I was twelve years old—in this very parlor. I hated every minute of it.

You even scolded me when I mouthed off at Mother." Then, Mark had been ungainly, his fleshy jowls tense with scorn, his abdomen pouching over belted shorts. Rather than procure a sitter for him, my parents had included him in their trips.

I nodded, that October afternoon again fresh in my memory. Stunned by Mark's words, I had leapt to Mother's defense. Her blue eyes were pained, brimming with tears. None of us had ever spoken to her like that, however much we'd wanted to. Dad looked on, helpless, and reached for another cigarette.

"Yes, I remember," I said, slipping my foot from my flats. "Also how Sister Landry happened to come by and remembered you from your Barat Hall days. How she took you to her classroom as a diversion so we could continue our visit—I also remember apologizing to you the next day. It was none of my business. But it left me wondering who you were."

Mark smiled, settled on the sofa, his backpack on the floor by his sandals. He was different now. Tall, slender in his sports shirt and slacks, his tapered fingers revealed an innate sensitivity. Most remarkable were his grey-green eyes that sought entrance into my world. I told him about my leave of absence from the Society. He was the first in my family to know.

Mark listened to my fears and then explained how to open a checking account, how to budget, pay bills, grocery shop, and other skills for managing on one's own, then assured me of his continuing support. I was astounded. My youngest brother had grown up. From Mother's letters over the years, it did not appear that would happen. Because few of his teachers knew how to engage his superior intelligence and sensitivity, he had floundered in many Catholic schools. Only during his junior year in Madrid, Spain, had he come alive to his true gifts. However my pride and low energy prevented further contacts with Mark, despite my discovery that temperamentally, we were alike.

Yes, I would miss Mark, especially now.

The morning of Dad's funeral Mass at Immaculata Church, Mother handed me her double-breasted white spring coat, trimmed with gold buttons and lined with silk.

"Here," she said in a flat tone. "You'll need this. It got cold during the night." No matter that the sleeves were too short, the shoulders snug. I needed the warmth, not having brought my coat from New Orleans.

During the limousine ride to Immaculata Church with Mother, chic in her dark coat and scarf, dry-eyed, she fingered her rosary beads and stared out the window. An abyss separated us. I wanted to reach out to her but feared she would rebuke me, so unlike her manner during yesterday's wake at Kriegshauser's.

Then, Mother had stood tall next to Dad's closed casket, which was covered by a spray of pink roses. Her simple black dress with long sleeves enhanced her grief. For hours, she received hugs and thanked everyone for coming, the same gracious way she sent guests home after one of her parties. Smells from other floral arrangements banking the walls of the double parlor produced a veritable death-garden. Small nieces and nephews, like skiffs, raced in and out of other parlors, "visiting the dead."

Exhausted by this cocktail-like atmosphere, I took frequent time-outs in the women's mirrored lounge, checked my watch—another gift from Mother from Maison Blanche, years before—and longed for the sofa bed in her family room where I was staying.

Atop the hill on Clayton Road, the parish church neared; above it, the cobalt sky ached with light, greening new trees and shrubs and grass. From the limousine, we watched somber pallbearers maneuver Dad's coffin from the hearse onto the dolly. Then someone opened the limousine door, the frosty air knifing me. I grimaced and followed Mother and the extended family through the great doors of the church and waited in the vestibule for the funeral cortege. It had been only six months since my total knee replacements, and I was too proud to carry my cane.

The funeral Mass was a blur of white-vested priests, hymns, candles, flowers, the Knights of Malta in their white capes and hats, sniffling worshippers, and eulogies. Next to me in the front pew sat Mother, rock-like, no tears. At times, something akin to grief tore within me, then subsided, then resurfaced. Still not understanding the dream of Dad's erection, my last visit with him in ICU consoled me. Somehow that had made up for a lifetime of mixed messages.

After the internment of Dad's remains in Calvary Cemetery, everyone gathered in my married brother's home in Warson Woods, a comfortable suburb in St. Louis County. Too exhausted to speak or to mill among the relatives that crammed every room, I joined Mother on the couch in the den, her blue eyes vacant, our emptied glasses of chardonnay on the coffee table in front of us. Still shivering, I snuggled into her white coat and tuned out the animated conversations swirling around me. These people seemed to have lives. I was still lost in mine.

In fantasy, I drifted back to my childhood pastime, rummaging through Mother's cedar chest. After pulling out my favorite dress, a coral one she had embroidered when pencil-slim before her pregnancies, I struggled into it, even forced my feet into her three-inch heels, then preened in front of her full-length mirror in hopes of becoming like her. Then I had had no identity. I still didn't. So sitting on that couch in her white spring coat, despite its not fitting just like that coral dress, I longed for her protection and care, strangely lavished upon me since I had left the convent. Evidence of her tastes abounded in my New Orleans apartment. Before returning there, I hung up Mother's coat in the hall closet, buoyed by my plan to return to St. Louis, my true home, or so I thought. Perhaps with Dad gone, Mother would be even more available to me. I could no longer manage on my own in New Orleans.

Within months, I had arranged my move to St. Louis. Dr. Kane and my supervisor at Associated Catholic Charities and my few friends supported my decision to help my newly widowed mother, although she had not asked for help. A strong-willed woman, she could fend for herself, except for loneliness that swamped her on Sundays, except for ineptness in traveling. That's where I would fit in.

15

Red Cardigan with Brass Buttons, November 12, 1980

It was the evening of my forty-fifth birthday. Soon I would meet Mother and my siblings and their spouses at Dominic's Restaurant on The Hill, an Italian-American enclave established in St. Louis by immigrants from Northern Italy and Sicily. Seated on my bed in the Frontenac Apartments in the Central West End, the Old World part of St. Louis, I methodically slipped on the red cardigan Mother had bought for me during our 1977 trip to Germany.

I still remembered the afternoon we visited Oberammergau, site of the Passion Play, in continuous performance since 1634, and then browsed the gift shop: unusual art works, clothing, candles, oversized books, cards, cattle bells affixed to leather strips, lined shelves and counters along the walls. A pine scent knifed the fresh air. Chilled to the bone, I followed Mother up and down the aisles, lest I lose my way among busloads of tourists pawing the wares. Diverse languages further disoriented me.

Suddenly, a red cardigan with brass buttons caught my attention. I stopped, fingered its thick wool. I wanted it badly, but its expense precluded using my money. I caught up to Mother and asked in a thin voice, "There's this sweater... It's perfect... Let me show it to you... Just what I've been looking for... It'll go with lots of my winter clothes." Once again, I reverted to my needy child, a tactic that had worked repeatedly, although I hated using it.

"Well, try it on. See if it fits," Mother said wearily, the tension in her voice disquieting me. Something was not right. Earlier that morning Mark, now living in Munich and studying German before pursing a doctorate in art history, had put us on the train, obviously relieved to be free of us.

After locating a mirror, I slipped off my jacket, then buttoned the sweater. It was perfect, its warmth cocooning my body.

Mother nodded. It had worked again.

Days passed. Mark's standoffish manner continued to make Mother anxious. One evening, sick with a headache, she excused herself from supper and retired to her room. For the first time, Mark and I were alone. From somewhere, saxophones droned; recessed lighting blurred harsh lines. Midway through our main course, with a bottle of chardonnay icing in a cooler, Mark leaned forward, his leather jacket enhancing broad shoulders toned by dance classes. His words flew at me. "Liz, just as you shared your plan to leave the convent with me, years ago, before telling the family, I want you to know that I'm gay—you're the first to know. Please keep this secret." A thin line of perspiration dotted his forehead, as he leaned against his armchair, anticipating my response.

"You may not believe this," I said, twisting a corner of my napkin in my lap, "but I sensed it all along. I'm honored you told me." Then I raised my glass and toasted him, the saxophones suddenly swelling. He smiled, then shared his painful search for his true orientation, beginning with sexual abuse from a neighbor when a boy, with humiliations in the open showers from Augustinian Brothers during high school, with discovery of his gay status at Holy Cross College, and his lovers in Munich.

So this was the source of tension between Mark and Mother. Sensing something amiss, she had planned this trip to bring him back to St. Louis. It failed. During the ride to the airport, she admitted she worried about him all the time.

In subsequent years, Mother continued glorying in Mark's achievements, gleaned from his letters; each one was an answer to her prayers. Rarely mentioned was my work with the Visiting Nurse Association, with my parish, the Jesuit-staffed St. Francis Xavier Church. More and more, Mark was becoming my rival, despite my carrying his secret.

I'd have to hurry or I'd be late. After fussing with my wavy brunette hair until it was just right, I pulled on my black leather boots, grabbed my coat, and headed to Dominic's to meet Mother and my married siblings.

A rush of hellos filled the entryway, as icy winds whipped the beribboned packages others carried.

We checked our coats in the cloakroom, then breathed deeply while scanning the restaurant. We'd been here before. Garlicky aromas, subdued lighting, oil paintings in gilded frames, starched tablecloths, napkins folded like birds of paradise, tucked in water goblets—yes, everything was the same, including romantic strains of violins seeping into this world of gourmet foods and pricey wines. Waiters in tuxes and busboys in wrap-around aprons served tables of moneyed patrons poring over leather-covered menus. We would soon join them.

Then the headwaiter escorted us to our reserved table, Mother in the lead. Trained to look good in public, I had trailed after her when a child, entering Our Lady of Lourdes Church, Sunday after Sunday, with my starched dress tied in the back, braids with matching ribbons, straw hat, white gloves, and my small purse with a nickel for the collection. Even then, I sensed it was a show, but I was still engulfed in the drama.

After the waiter took our drink orders, we settled in our over-stuffed armchairs, twiddled with the array of silverware at each place. It would be a three-hour supper, as always.

"I just had this letter from Mark!" Mother exclaimed over the awkward silence around the table. Pulling it from her purse, she read parts of it. "He's just had one of his poems published—talks also about his dance class and the next performance with his company—still studying German at the university. However, he also talks about moving to a warmer climate, like Barcelona. So many interests," she sighed, searching for our admiration, "I can't keep up with him." Then she returned her letter to her purse and looked blank. I sensed everyone's thirst for the drink orders. I shared it.

How these recitals irked me. Yet I dared not displease her. No one did.

Then I spotted our waiter carrying a tray full of drinks. Relief lifted the tense mood. As soon as each was served, stories buzzed around me. Unable to keep up, I listened: my brother Tom's sarcasm, a carryover from childhood, and his wife's efforts to smooth over his insults; my brother John's businesslike tone and his wife Susie's enthusiasm; my sister Martha's quick repartee and her husband's raucous laughter.

With subsequent drink orders, especially after the third round, comments flew helter-skelter. Sitting at my accustomed place at Mother's right, looking handsome in my red sweater but feeling miserable, I continued sipping fruity wines and buttering warm rye rolls. No one ever asked how I was or what I did between such gatherings.

Yet, remembering my Dale Carnegie course in communications I had taken in New Orleans, how people loved to talk about themselves, I raised questions that drew lengthy responses from my family. I hoped such questions would spawn others directed toward me, but they did not.

Then came the moment everyone anticipated. Waiters encircled our table, their gloved hands placing our entrées, covered by silver globes, at our places. At a given signal, the waiters snapped them up, immediately releasing savory aromas. Then began serious eating with little conversation save for how tasty this or that was, or an exchange of morsels placed on butter plates. Invariably, Mother's displeasure with her beef tenderloin silenced everyone, until someone helped her over the disappointment. By that time, wines had mellowed me into the pastoral scene in the painting hanging across from me. Then birthday gifts, Irish coffees, and dessert remained before the awkward moments over the bill; it was usually three hundred dollars or more, an amount that perplexed Mother, until one of my brothers verified the total and she signed the charge slip. After weaving toward the cloakroom to retrieve our coats, we exchanged hugs and thanks in sharp winds outside the restaurant while waiting for our cars.

Elizabeth

Later, seated on my bed, dizzy with wine, I unbuttoned my red cardigan, carefully placed it in its protective bag, and stashed it in my dresser until the next special occasion Mother would organize. Not knowing when that would occur, I simply endured my life, spliced by regular office visits with my rheumatologist and his drugs that kept me half-sick, my knees a trainwreck. Thus I continued floundering with no true identity save the social-worker façade I wore five days each week.

I still keep the red cardigan in its plastic bag but now wear it for ordinary occasions, glad that my life is finally ordinary. That, however, took years to happen.

16

Orthopedic Shoes, June 1984

"You might want to see my podiatrist, Dr. Feldhauer," Mother said over Sunday supper at Cheshire Inn, our glasses of chardonnay almost empty, the remnants of our roast beef dinners lining our plates. "He can evaluate your feet and recommend orthotics, if you need them." She was right. I had to do something. For months, hammertoes had rubbed against the tops of my shoes, making my gait even more hazardous. And for months she had told me about her orthopedic shoes called Barefoot Freedoms, worn because of bunions caused, years before, by walking in three-inch heels. She used to say, laughing, "Back then, no one would think of leaving their front doors without wearing three-inch heels. That's what everyone did. Even when I took you kids for walks."

She was right. Within a few weeks, I, too, was wearing orthotics in Barefoot Freedoms, navy like hers; with the flaps, an extra, they looked like brogues.

Elizabeth

Would that a simple corrective device could assuage my yearning for a significant male. Given my continuing discomfort around sexually active men, I was glad my forays into the Catholic singles world had been fruitless. As a safe substitute, I turned to Bill Hutchison, Jesuit, then dean of the School of Social Work at St. Louis University. He'd directed my retreat the year before at the Passionist Retreat Center. Sundays, after Mass at St. Francis Xavier, we met in the seclusion of his office for spiritual direction, all the while keeping my agenda under wraps. His quiet manner welcomed my insights from meditations on the gospels, insights on homilies we'd just heard. Of my health, we rarely spoke. Yet these flights into spiritual realms mimicked some kind of relationship, despite worsening knee pain that plunged me deeper into denial of my body; invisible, it only materialized in my bathroom mirror.

"Liz, with your love for solitude and prayer, would you consider making another directed retreat next summer?" Bill asked one snowy morning. Outside his chilly office, ice pellets spit upon the floor-to-ceiling windows. We were ending another hour of direction, a coffee table separating our leather armchairs. His bulky cardigan, of Goodwill vintage, opened to a plaid sports shirt, khakis. His question intrigued me. I leaned forward in my chair, shoving my fists into the sleeves of my coat. I used to view such retreats, based upon the abbreviated *Spiritual Exercises of St. Ignatius*, as a relic of my former life behind cloister doors.

"Have you any suggestions?" I asked.

He brightened, shifting in his chair. "I sure do. The New England Province of Jesuits has a retreat center outside of Boston. In Gloucester. Right on the ocean. It's called Gonzaga—Eastern Point." A deep smile creased his clean-shaven jaws. "I made my retreat there last year. I'll never forget it. Something about that ocean, its varied moods, the stillness."

Immediately, I was intrigued.

"You're going where?" Mother said in response to my retreat plan when I called her. "By yourself? But that's so far from home. What if you get into trouble? Who'll help you?" Two years before, bed-bound with a bad back and complications from drugs prescribed by my rheumatologist, I had convalesced in her condo for a month. She had seen me at my lowest.

"Somehow I'll manage," I said, miffed by her apprehensions. "This is something I must do. I'll ask for help if I need to." She knew little of the multiple demons hounding me.

The TWA flight to Boston's Logan International Airport was uneventful, as was locating a limousine for the one-hour drive to Gloucester and the retreat center. Swinging onto Niles Pond Road, overarched by oaks and maples, I gasped. Everywhere one looked, there was sunlit beauty. Ocean-washed air murmured through wild grasses, evergreens, birches, and in the circle drive of the main stone house, expansive limbs of the copper-leafed beech tree welcomed me.

Outside the office was a list of the retreatants and their assigned rooms in the adjoining wing. It looked as if fifty others would also be meeting daily with their directors for the next eight days. Still dazed by my new surroundings, I checked off my name, then lugged my suitcase to my room, glad for the support of my orthopedic shoes. The logistics of this complex required much walking.

My spartan room had a casement window overlooking the ocean: its furnishings, a bed, a desk and chair, and a washstand;

its walls, watery green; its flooring, squares of tan linoleum tile. Much later, I learned the Jesuits had built this wing in 1957 to accommodate their high school and college students for weekend retreats, as well as to attract vocations to their community. In the aftermath of the Vatican II renewal, however, the retreat center was open to all persons wishing time and space apart from their busy lives.

My breathing fluttered as I made my bed and settled in. Soon animated conversations echoed along the corridor outside my room. It sounded like nuns. It never occurred to me to introduce myself, despite being apart from the Society for ten years. I was already in retreat, I told myself, even though the retreat's silence would begin only after the evening meeting in the fireside room. In the hour before supper, I sat by the ocean, glorying in gulls screeching, alighting on Brace Rock, glorying in the pull of the tides on the surf, glorying in my at-oneness within this vast world. Bill had been right about this place, and the adventure was just beginning.

A gong broke into my reverie, announcing supper. Pushing myself off the boulder, I picked my way across the expanse of sun-bleached grass to the dining room. Approaching the entrance, I was taken aback by chattering retreatants, standing in clusters, many nursing glasses of wine. Immediately, I spotted boxes of Gallo wine, red and white, on the serving table, then filled a glass; its tangy sweetness mellowed me.

"All the way from St. Louis? How did you hear of this place?" a jolly nun in a black habit asked, fingering the profession cross around her neck. Uncomfortable with small talk, I took another sip of wine and satisfied her curiosity, then moved back to the serving table for a refill. While listening to conversations buzzing around me, I discovered priests, brothers, nuns (some wearing habits), and graduate students from the Weston School of Theology, another Jesuit-sponsored institution. Everyone seemed to know one another.

Uncomfortable minutes followed until the spaghetti dinner was served. I was among the first to fill my plate and sat before the windows facing the ocean. More retreatants settled around me, their excitement annoying, as they continued the "Do you know...?" or "Were you there?" games. Occasionally I smiled as if interested, but could not wait to return to my room. The ocean breezes chilled me.

Later, gathered with the retreatants and staff in the fireside room, I met my director, Sister Mary Assunta Boyle, matronly in her striped blouse, skirt, and sandals. Wavy grey hair framed her pallid face. Despite her warm welcome and assurances of help, inwardly I groused. I had hoped one of the Jesuits, tall, bearded, and fit in pullover sweaters, standing around the sides of the room, would direct my retreat.

At my scheduled time for direction the next morning, I knocked on the opened door of one of the parlors in the main house. Inside sat Sister Assunta, the Bible on her lap filled with markers. Outdoors, clouds filled with moisture mirrored the gloom in my heart.

"Come in, Liz," Sister said, brightening. "Take whatever chair that will be most comfortable. I see you pray with the *Jerusalem Bible* too."

Already she had sized me up. Settling myself opposite her, I opened my notebook and readied my pen.

"Good morning, Sister," I said, feigning a smile. "It's good to be here, to experience the ocean like this. Very soothing throughout the night." I did not tell her of the snoring nun in the room next to me, nor of the noisy commodes in the common bathroom down the corridor. Sister Assunta's toothy smile stretched thin lips.

"Sounds like you've made a good beginning. Perhaps you'd like to know about me. For years I've been helping the Jesuits direct retreats here. It's always a joy to be invited back." Then she spoke glowingly of her New York community, their implementation of the Vatican II reforms and varied ministries. I squirmed under her recital, still shamed by having walked away from the Society years before. I still did not know how to be a woman who was beyond aping Mother's behaviors. I knew they did not fit me.

"Now that you know a little about me," Sister added in vigorous tones, "Let me hear of your experiences in prayer, what you hope to gain from this retreat. That'll help me, as well." With a dry mouth, I skimmed over the highlights of my life, paying scant attention to my years in the Society. She was right about my use of the *Jerusalem Bible*, when I was focused enough to meditate at home.

"Liz, you're in the right place. For the next eight days, let the ocean quiet you. Allow the immensity of God's love to penetrate every cell in your being. You'll not be disappointed." A mysterious light suddenly fired her dark eyes. I knew she was right. "Should you wish to meditate, you might begin with the creation story in Genesis. See yourself in it. Or go to the Psalms. The same thing. Above all, relax. Leave St. Louis behind. Be here fully." She smiled deeply. I did, too. "Until tomorrow, then, the same time," she added as I collected my things.

Amazingly the days passed, Sister's welcome warming my resistance in following her direction. Never had I prayed as I had here, this true home for my soul. Of little importance were several sea storms that rattled my casement windows and set off the foghorn at the Gloucester lighthouse, that shrouded the ocean from view. Days of pristine sunshine soon followed, like the first morning of creation. I had been washed clean. Already, I was anticipating next year's directed retreat in this sacred place.

The last afternoon of the retreat, while sitting next to the ocean, haunting melodies seized me. In the distance, a lean bronzed man with T-shirt, cut-offs, and sandals stepped gingerly over mounds of granite boulders, playing his heart into a Native American flute. His antics reminded me of the fiddler in *The Fiddler on the Roof*; like him, this man was totally absorbed in his music-making, totally enveloped in the ocean-and-sky-world. I could not take my eyes off him and followed him until he could no longer be seen.

I later learned this man was Richard Stanley, the Jesuit director of this center. He had just returned from a needed break. In 2001 our paths would again cross when he began directing my retreats at Eastern Point. In the interim years, parish and hospital work had absorbed his energies.

The morning of my return flight to St. Louis, I laced my orthopedic shoes, tears stinging my eyes, then repacked my bag and cleaned up my room for the next retreatant. Home meant Mother and more Sundays.

17

Second Wedding Gown,
January 17, 1987

Years passed, enveloped in Mother's growing solicitude that further destabilized me, although I made efforts to separate from her. Often she remarked on my limp, my ashen color, my lack of energy. I sloughed off her concerns, all the while knowing arthritic pain was having a field day in my body, despite drugs prescribed by my rheumatologist. In 1985, the prosthesis in my right knee failed, requiring another total knee replacement. Its surgery and convalesence interrupted a renewed relationship with Joe Gummersbach, a recent widower.

It had all seemed so odd: Joe's immediate attraction to me after twenty-four years. I still remember the barbecue friends gave to reintroduce us. It was July 1984, a steamy evening, seven months after Joe had lost Marge, his wife, to pneumonia. The ground shook beneath me as I walked into the sunroom, filled with guests, and felt that same passion in his amber eyes as I had when much younger.

"Hi, Liz," he stammered, extending his hand to me. In his other was a perspiring Manhattan. Meticulously groomed in a navy and white seersucker suit, shirt and tie, he still looked the same, except for thinning hair and a protruding abdomen. "Great to see you again," he added. "It's been a long time." Conversations paused around us, then resumed, our moment of meeting swallowed within the festivities.

I mumbled something, then greeted the other guests, including his mother and priest brother, Jim. I was suddenly very hot in my ivory cotton sundress and red sandals. Sipping the chilled wine helped.

All during the evening, Joe hung around me, nervously plying me with details of his life, just as he had in the 1950s: his marriage to Marge; their efforts to have a child; their life in Arlington Heights, Illinois, where he had held a mid-management position in a supply company; his retirement and relocation to St. Louis to oversee his mother's finances. For some reason, Joe still needed my affirmation. Only rarely did he raise questions about my life. Only much later did I learn of his wife's addiction to martinis: her way of managing severe premenstrual syndrome, despite years of ineffective drugs that had depressed her immune system.

The evening wound down with my cleaning up the kitchen with others, Joe still at my elbow, dishtowel in hand. Following me to the door, he again extended his hand, his Holy Cross ring mashing my fingers, just as it had years before in those darkened movie theaters.

Feverishly, he said, "Liz, it's been great seeing you again. When I get home from my trip with Jim, I'll give you a call. We'll be in Vancouver for two weeks."

"I'd like that," I said, afire with excitement.

Elizabeth

Many nights, sexual tensions wired me, fueled my fantasies, as I thrashed atop my bed. Motorists whizzed by on the street below; occasional flashing lights from emergency vehicles traversed the walls of my bedroom. Desperate for sleep, I finally resorted to masturbation. It helped.

"Would you like to picnic at Maramec Spring Park? Next Saturday?" Joe asked upon his return. "If you've not been there, I'd love to show it to you. It's a long drive, down Interstate 44, but worth it. Just east of St. James." Eagerly I accepted his invitation and offered to bring a hamper of food and drinks.

At ten o'clock, the doorbell rang. It was Joe. This time, Mother was not around to answer. A last check in my bedroom mirror—I did look smart in a brown plaid shirt, khakis, and red sandals—I hurried to the door, hoping he'd not notice my limp.

"Hi, Liz," Joe said, his face flushing. "You look terrific! Here, let me carry that," he added reaching for the hamper. "If we get a move on it, we can beat the storms coming from the west."

Joe's Buick ate up miles while he spoke, nonstop, of his earlier work as salesman with B. Herder Book Company which had kept him on the road, more about Marge and her miscarriage, of his hopes for the St. Louis Cardinals football team, which had finished in third place last year. Although inundated by this information, I pretended to listen. Of more concern were threatening skies and turbulent winds. However, on the turnoff to Highway 195, my anticipation heightened.

"We're finally here," Joe said, flipping off the ignition. "Looks like we have the park pretty much to ourselves. How about a walk? There's lots to see here," he added. I'd hoped we'd just picnic on the benches and while away the afternoon until time to drive home, or something like that. Certainly not walking. That was too exhausting. However, my need to please Joe overrode the pain in my knees. He needn't know about my rheumatoid arthritis; not yet.

The afternoon unfolded into a nightmare: our long walk along the trail bordering the springs; the thunderstorm breaking over us and our seeking shelter under a pavilion; our mad dash back to his car, hand in hand, both soaking wet; ham sandwiches and Cokes from the hamper in Joe's car, still buffeted by winds and pelted with rain; more of Joe's life experiences. Later, it puzzled me that he'd not asked about my convent years, especially why I'd left, or about my years as a single woman with a career. Still, there was a man in my life.

Later, seated across from Joe in my kitchen, we finished the remnants in the hamper. Of no matter that our clothes were still damp, our hair tousled, my face pale without makeup. We planned our next date, supper on Maryland Plaza in the Central West End. Before leaving, Joe kissed me on the cheek, his eyes ablaze. I did not sleep that night.

The ground continued shaking as we dated. More suppers enlivened by Manhattans and chardonnay, followed by intimacies shared in my bedroom. Occasional break-ups heightened this drama that seemed to point toward marriage. But I was not sure. Certainly Joe was a good man, but we had little in common, except expensive tastes internalized from our families. Besides, his efforts to support me during another surgery for a failed total knee replacement and convalescence had annoyed me. And the moment I unlocked my kitchen door from my day's work at DePaul Hospital, the phone was ringing. It was always Joe. At times I let the phone ring. More than ever, I needed space from him. Yet I prayed for some sign, because his ardor only deepened.

Elizabeth

It came the night of June 24, 1986, during a curious dream:

I am suspended in total darkness as velvet strips caress my naked body. Then a blinding light envelops Joe and me, our combined energies, ecstatic, as we exclaim "Yes" to each other. Darkness then eclipses this vision. Again, I'm alone.

Stunned by the dream, I sat up on the side of my bed and hugged my swollen knees and reentered the dream experience. It seemed to indicate marriage with Joe: a union of body, mind, and spirit within the mystery of God. Later, Joe was ecstatic hearing my dream and my acceptance of his proposal.

However, we never actualized those depths, distracted by the hectic planning for our wedding. In Mother's hands it became a society wedding, rather than the simple one we'd planned. "Why, you can't get married like that!" she had said, sitting in her family room the July afternoon when we shared our engagement. "What would my sisters and brothers think? How much I wish your father were here to help me with this!" she added, pouting, twisting her wedding ring on her finger. It would be as she said.

And it was. During the months preceding our wedding I noticed Joe's swelling abdomen, his shadowed eyes, his passivity, but said nothing. Suddenly I was making all the decisions. The purchase of a spacious condo in the Lindell Terrace in the Central West End and its decoration presaged the reality to come. Combining our furniture and other effects into #7A terrified me. Other than keeping house, I knew nothing about being a wife, despite following a theology of marriage course at St. Louis University. A whirl of parties and gifts further disoriented me. But last summer's dream of our ecstatic "Yes!" prodded me toward our scheduled January commitment, applauded by our families and friends.

The morning of our wedding Mass in Our Lady's Chapel at the St. Louis Cathedral, the sky was overcast, with stinging winds and ice-slushed streets. As prearranged, a Westrich photographer took pictures of Mother adjusting the silk taffeta streamers on the back of my ivory lace sheath gown while sitting on the bed I would soon share with Joe. In one of the pictures I saw much later, a hesitant smile masked my annoyance at her dressing me again. Again we'd shopped at Montaldo's, and again, I looked like a bride doll, only this time awaiting a human Prince Charming. Behind me, on the dresser, sat Joe's gold-framed photo, his engaging smile just the same as in college when I had first met him.

A white stretch limousine transported Mother and me the few blocks to the St. Louis Cathedral. Our guests were already seated in the chapel, redolent with freesias, lilies, and peach roses adorning the sanctuary and marble altar; it felt like a chilly mausoleum. I dreaded what was to come. Hurriedly, I pinned the wreath of stephanotis over my brunette pageboy and went to meet Joe in the sacristy. Boyishly, he grinned, his new navy pinstripe suit masking an even larger abdomen. I lowered my eyes, barely breathing. It was time. Again remembering last summer's dream, I took his arm and followed the white-vested priests into the chapel. No one was giving me away.

After the entrance procession, led by guitarists and vocalists, the drama escalated with scriptural readings, a sermon, and hymns, and then our exchange of vows, witnessed by the pastor, Msgr. Roland Gannon. But my heart was someplace else. As with other vows I had taken as a nun, this was something I had to do, despite not knowing why. Yet I played the role of the happy bride, and Joe loved me for it. So did family and friends kneeling behind us.

Whisked in the stretch limousine to our reception, I froze as Joe inched his arm around my shoulders. I had no words. Nor did he. We stared out the windows at passing motorists.

That changed as we caught our guests' merriment on the twenty-first floor of the University Club. We both knew how to please, and we assumed the smiles of the freshly married as featured in slick bridal magazines. The smiles continued in lengthy poses before the Westrich photographer in the glass-enclosed foyer banked with ferns and fig trees.

Then into the private dining room, tables set for eight, elegant with white cloths over forest green underskirts and napkins; centerpieces with more freesias, lilies, and peach roses. A pianist played near the open bar. Still more camera shots with Joe and our families, while our guests smiled and toasted us. Many had never experienced such a spiritual wedding, especially the prayer to Our Lady I had composed and recited with Joe at the end of Mass, an accustomed ritual following Catholic weddings. Perhaps through such prayer, Joe and I would find our way. At least I hoped so.

In retrospect, Joe and I did have a moment of soul sharing, during our retreat in Gloucester the following summer. I had preferred going alone as usual, but he insisted upon joining me. After several days of quiet prayer, we drove to Essex for a fish dinner. It was evening. Joe could barely talk. "Liz," he said, "The Holy Cross brother directing my retreat suggested I pray with the ocean—I did what he said—I found myself cupping waters from the surf, blessing it. Then I opened my fingers and watched the waters again become one with the ocean. I still feel giddy." Joe breathed deeply and sipped his Manhattan.

"I'm glad for you, Joe," I said. That was the first time I'd glimpsed his soul, until then crimped by rote prayers from his Catholic upbringing. Never again did I catch this beauty.

Chilled chardonnay at our table relaxed me somewhat, but I was ever leery because I felt the photographer's flash made it imperative that I appear happy. Evidently it worked, because the photos in the wedding album reveal the same sweet smile of the bride doll and her beloved. Joe and I had little to say, other than commenting on the tasty filet of beef entrée, toasting each other for the photographer's camera, and passing condiments to others at our table.

Because there was no receiving line, it would have been fitting had Joe and I visited each table and thanked our guests for sharing our special day. But that thought never occurred to me. I wanted only to get out of that elegant place that was choking me, and, still more, get out of the wedding dress as soon as possible. After quick goodbyes to our mothers, we left for our flight to San Francisco and our honeymoon at The Huntingdon on Nob Hill.

It was after midnight when Joe and I claimed our small room; its full-sized bed, with a cigarette hole in the red quilted bedspread, precluded our sleeping together. Only the king-sized bed in his apartment had accommodated us the one time we had slept together. Awkward moments passed, juiced by dry champagne friends had ordered for us. Too exhausted to make other arrangements, we settled in, pulled the covers to our chins, and waited for the release of sleep.

Within moments, Joe began snoring, thrashing upon the bed. Rather than land upon the floor, I grabbed my pillow, retreated into the bathroom, lined the narrow tub with Turkish towels, and tried to sleep. However, the absurdity of my position only fueled more annoyance.

Home one week later, I suggested we seek marital counseling from several therapists we'd considered. Joe appeared motivated to do so, but failed to make the appointment for us. Because I did not want to go alone, I dropped it. Never did it occur to me to seek help for myself. That did not happen until I began working with Ellen Scheire, a Zurich-trained Jungian analyst, the following year.

After Joe and I divorced in 1990, my ivory lace-wedding gown donated to The Miriam Shop, Mother groused over our four-thousand-dollar wedding. I never reminded her of the simple one Joe and I had planned, but it had turned out to be an expensive lesson for me as well. I was suffocating in her elegant world and in the one Joe offered me, devoid of engagement on any level. Separate incomes had kept us comfortable but isolated. I desperately needed my own space, but it would take more years before I actualized it.

Part 4

Glimmerings of Change,
1991–2000

18

White Blouse with Lace-Trimmed Collar, September 16, 1991

Our spacious marital condo, still on the market, echoed with emptiness. In my trousseau nightgown, I sat on my unmade bed, listlessly staring out the narrow window. The mid-morning sun warmed a city pigeon squatting on the sill, preening her slate-grey feathers. I became one with her, then flopped back upon pillows and shut my eyes. Bronchitis, joint pain, and low-grade fever had prompted my calling in sick for work, unusual because of my compulsion to hoard sick time for possible surgeries on my joints, still swollen and inflamed.

Then a recurring dream hounded me.

Joe and I argue violently. We've been drinking. I hit him in the mouth, bite him, then lock myself in the bathroom. I'm terrified, exhausted, my body filled with pain ... I sit on the commode, sobbing.

I hugged my shoulders, rolled over on my side. There was no point recording this dream in my notebook, a practice I'd adopted as a result of entering Jungian analysis with Ellen Sheire. We'd looked at similar ones during our hours together, but I could not identify with them. My drinking had stopped years before, on August 25, 1988. That night, Joe and I had dined in Queen Anne's Restaurant in Chatham, Cape Cod, before driving up to Gloucester for our retreat. Frosty silence kept us on edge until the waiter brought us our drinks. My eight-ounce goblet of Zinfandel Blush precluded my ordering a second that had always put me in the flowers. Its bouquet and bubbly smoothness tantalized me; to make it last longer, I added ice chips from my water glass. Around us, animated conversations buzzed while we waited for our entrées and nursed our drinks. Imperceptibly, a sinister force hardened my heart, and witch-like, I began spewing venom upon Joe, slowly at first, until our waiter served us. All the while, Joe said nothing, sipped his Manhattan, cut into his beef tenderloin. His passivity fueled even more venom. I could not stop. It felt like someone yelling through me, a yelling that escalated in the parking lot and during the drive to our rented cottage. Never had I behaved that way, and I knew it. Later, severe dehydration, sweats, and frequent trips to the bathroom filled the night, a hell of my own making. The next morning's hangover convinced me to quit drinking. Yet I had remained miserable for years and did not know why.

Often, Ellen had heard that story and subsequent ones, marked by seething resentments and self-pity. Seated across from her in her Montclair apartment in the Central West End one afternoon, I still remember her saying, "Liz, it sounds to me like you're in a dry drunk. Your dreamer thinks so too." She dropped her usual happy demeanor, which, for months I'd thought was a ploy to keep me in analysis, and her brown eyes firmed, her round cheeks tensed. Then she laid her writing board on the carpet and leaned toward me. Immediately, I shut down, having no clue of what she was talking about. I sucked my tongue, noted a striking canvas on the wall opposite me, something she likely had purchased during the twenty years she had practiced as an analyst in Vienna before moving to St. Louis in 1986. Ellen was on to me.

On a hunch, I flipped open my notebook to the 1989 Family Program at Edgewood Hospital, a treatment facility for alcoholism, again Ellen's recommendation. Repeatedly, I'd written that alcoholism was a family disease; faulty perceptions, denial, and rationalization sickened everyone's spirits, steeped in self-pity and resentments. Slowly memories from my First Holy Communion brunch and others over the long years began dispelling my fog. Dewar's scotch had been the lubricant of those Moloney and Costigan gatherings, filled with guffaws, Irish jokes, slurred banter, unsteady gaits. Yet none of my relatives—physicians, lawyers, businessmen in suits and ties—looked like the homeless drunks I had seen from the back seat of Dad's car, passing through North St. Louis on the way to Sportsmen's Park for Cardinals games when I was a child. And then there was that night in Queen Anne's restaurant with Joe.

Again I flopped back upon the pillows. Perhaps I was an alcoholic. Repeated efforts to workshop my way through depression and relationship problems had failed. All that was left was Ellen's repeated recommendation, Alcoholics Anonymous. There were meetings in an old three-story brownstone just across the street. For years, I'd noticed drunks in suits and ties joining their friends and hurrying up the marble steps around noontime. If I hurried, I could make it. I would dress up for the occasion. I must look good for this new venture.

Elizabeth

Standing in front of the bedroom mirror, I buttoned my new white blouse with the lace-trimmed collar, Mother's latest purchase at Dillard's Department Store after we'd had an early Sunday supper. Then I tied on my khaki wrap-around skirt, slipped on my flats, and took a final look in the mirror. My feverish brown eyes gave me away. Would AA help me find a way out of my madness, laced with alcohol that still surfaced during birthday suppers with Mother and my siblings? During the last one held at Tony's, old family stories had waxed with each round of drinks. With permission of Dad's ICU doctor, Mother had spooned ice chips saturated with Dewar's scotch onto his parched tongue. Because alcoholism was a family disease, maybe Ellen had been right about my being a dry drunk. She called it a disease. I would soon find out.

After pulling myself up the banister of the brownstone, I followed others into the long meeting room, its walls and ceilings begrimed by years of cigarette smoke. Ill-matched tables and chairs spanned its length. Window units wheezed frigid air. Tears in the stained all-weather carpet gave me pause as I sank into an armchair. Around me, all kinds of people smiled and laughed, an enviable lightness in their eyes. Never had I been so lonely. I coughed, sneezed, buried my head in my Kleenex. Suddenly, I felt overdressed in my white blouse with the lace trim. I ached to get out of there, to return to bed and not become sicker from the cigarette smoke. More merriment filled the room as stragglers filled vacant chairs around the tables. Some munched sandwiches and sipped coffee.

Then a cab driver with a black tie leaned over my shoulder, handed me a placard, and asked, "Welcome to our meeting! I'm Jim. Will you please read 'How It Works' from the *Big Book of Alcoholics Anonymous*?" I was stuck.

The room quieted after he rapped the gavel and asked for silence, then opened the meeting with the Serenity Prayer: "God grant me the serenity to accept the things I cannot change, the courage to change the things I can, and the wisdom to know the difference." Around me, voices melded into one: solemn, haunting. I listened, mashing my toes against my flats. Again the ground was shaking. A pregnant pause followed, many sitting straighter in their chairs, some with pens poised over notebooks. Then my new friend smiled and nodded to me.

In a hoarse voice, I began reading aloud, certain everyone knew this was my first AA meeting. One sentence pierced me to the core: "There are those, too, who suffer grave emotional and mental disorders, but many of them do recover if they have the capacity to be honest." So it was about honesty. Somehow I finished reading, "...that God could and would (relieve our alcoholism) if He were sought." Everyone murmured thanks, some lit another cigarette. The solemn tone in the room deepened. More than ever, I retreated to my inner world and longed for the privacy of home, but self-respect glued me to my armchair. Besides, my knees needed a respite before recrossing Lindell Boulevard.

Announcements and meditation from a grey book followed. Then the meeting was open for sharing. Barely was there a moment between stories reminding me of a jeweled kaleidescope; each one was tinged with darkness, but shot through with an uncanny light. With all my heart, I wanted what they had. I was, like them, an alcoholic. I would join them in the cleansing fire that was changing their lives, in the laughter still rocking in the room. Suddenly my new blouse and the sham it represented lost its hold upon me.

Before leaving, I learned of a non-smoking meeting I could attend the following morning before work. Then I could announce, however hesitantly, "My name is Liz. I'm an alcoholic." And see what would follow. Ellen would be happy with this development.

That night, restless in bed, I was concerned lest my voice fail me during tomorrow's meeting. Years of compromise to Mother's control had diminished it. Perhaps if I rehearsed something—two sentences at least, as I had during my analysis with Dr. Kane. Then, I had begun small, until I recovered my full voice, hearing it fill shadowy confines of his office. While shuffling words around, I fell asleep.

Then a dream shocked me. It was two-thirty a.m.

It is a balmy summer evening. I decide to walk on Lindell Boulevard in front of my condo and enjoy the sunset. In a dreamy manner, I glory in the brilliant sky, the soft winds fanning my face. Then I trip on a crack in the sidewalk and fall. Hard. Panic seizes me. I discover I'm naked. Passersby gawk. No one offers to help me to my feet. Because of my artificial knee joints, I cannot get up. I sit there, my knees drawn to my chest.

I pulled myself up on the side of my bed, my head throbbing, as I recorded the dream in my journal. I needed help, but had to ask for it. I thought my artful dressing had fooled everyone. It had all been a lie.

I grabbed the phone and called Ellen. "Can we talk?" I blurted. We did for the next hour.

At dawn, new resolve fired my lethargy as I dressed, break-fasted, and crossed Lindell Boulevard for my second AA meeting. Regulars, coffee mugs in hands, newspapers under their arms, greeted their friends and shared more stories. But unlike yesterday, these regulars were mostly men, about thirty of them, dressed in sharp suits and ties, wearing polished shoes. Among them sat three women in cotton dresses and heels, rubbing sleep out of their eyes. Alarmed by the predominantly masculine presence filling the room, I slunk in my chair, fingered the buckle on my skirt, and desperately held on to the two sentences I had prepared earlier this morning. I must speak, despite my terror of men.

The meeting began. Again I was asked to read "How It Works," my voice echoing against the fourteen-foot ceiling. After the meditation from *The Daily Reflections*, the chairperson invited comments. Like yesterday, everyone jumped in, made light of fears that used to cripple them, interfaced by new behaviors learned through the practice of the 12 Steps. Somehow, they were central to this way of living. Again my heart was afire. Urgent was my need to share. Thirty-five minutes into the meeting, I caught an opening, spoke up, "Hi, I'm Liz. I'm an alcoholic."

Everyone turned toward me, smiles brightening their faces, exclaiming in one voice, "Hi Liz! Welcome! Glad you came back!" I sunk in my seat, their enthusiasm swamping my two sentences. No one had ever been that excited over me. None knew the gloomy places where I had lived out my entire life. The room was silent. Everyone was waiting. Desperately, I sought words, any words, sought escape in the apple tree in the side yard framed by the oversized window in front of me. Then, my voice quivering like Jell-O, I said, "I don't know what to say—I'm glad to be here—I'll come back tomorrow."

Again everyone thanked me with the same enthusiasm. They knew I was a newcomer and wanted me back. Among them, I would learn to dress myself from the inside out. I had made a critical beginning, thanks to Ellen's persistence. She knew me like none other.

The white blouse with the lace-trimmed collar hung in my closet, jammed among other apparel. It represented years of hiding out beneath elegant clothing and accessories reflecting Mother's tastes, believing their allure masked years of shame and guilt; it also represented my need to drink elegant wines, becoming airborne, thereby escaping the truth of who I really was. AA began to open chinks in my denial and rationalization, as had my analysis with Dr. Kane, years before. I would find my true voice, but needed help. Something deep within yearned for wholeness and would not be quieted.

19

Beige Silk Suit,
May 1, 1993

Mother was smartly dressed in navy slacks and striped jacket, awaiting my arrival at the front entrance of the Hanley Tower Condominium, banked with holly trees and boxwood hedges. It was the afternoon of Mark's graduation Mass at Aquinas Institute during which he would receive a master's degree in pastoral studies. In 1988 he had returned to St. Louis, fresh from a conversion experience while visiting Montserrat, the Benedictine monastery in Barcelona, Spain. In subsequent years, he sought entrance into a comparable one in the States, but found none suitable. Still perceiving himself a servant of the Church, he then studied theology in preparation for the lay ministry, studies financed by Mother.

Pulling up the circular drive, I watched the doorman escort Mother to my car, then open the door. High color flushed her sagging jowls. No one would suspect she was on medication for a new heart condition.

"Is that a new outfit?" Mother asked, following a buss on my cheek. Often, she had asked that question now that I was buying my clothes. She seemed surprised at my emerging taste, my youthful appearance. Now eighty-four years old, she was slowing down, her narrow shoulders slightly stooped.

"No, I bought it at the Clare-Joseph Outlet Store for Tall Women on Hampton Avenue—a few years ago. I've worn it before," I said checking my watch. A beige silk suit with a cropped jacket and flared skirt looked lovely with my ivory blouse.

"Well, my memory's not as good as it used to be," she added with a rueful smile, fingering the blue beads Mark had recently given her, a decided departure from the expensive jewelry she usually wore. Then she added, "Do you like my new earrings? Blue ones to match these beads. From Mark—this morning. He knows I like small ones." That was the rub. He knew how to ply her with gifts, whereas mine were rarely used. Suddenly very warm, I turned on the car's air conditioner, then accelerated onto Hanley Road.

For years, my jealousy and envy had festered beneath contrived smiles in the company of Mother and her favorite son. Not only did Mark usurp her affections, but he displayed unusual brilliance during family gatherings in four-star restaurants she arranged. Immediate recall of theater, film, dance, music, and architecture, experienced during his travels abroad, evidenced his encyclopedic mind. Also fluent in Spanish, Italian, German, and French, he nuanced subtleties, otherwise lost to me. His boundless energy also piqued my self-loathing. It was all I could do to get through each day.

Beige Silk Suit, May 1, 1993

The chapel used by Aquinas Institute for the graduation Mass was claustrophobic with hooded black-gowned graduates, their red tassels swinging from mortarboards, with white-habited Dominicans, some with swirling black capes, preparing the altar for the Mass. Mark stood tall among them, caught up in the drama. The air was stale. Guests, atwitter like sparrows, hugged friends in the vestibule, giggled, poured down the aisles into the pews, then fanned themselves with programs. It would be a long afternoon.

Suddenly a rousing hymn stirred my malaise. The Mass was beginning. I stood, picked up the program, like others around me, but only mouthed the words. I had no energy. Prayers and readings from scripture followed. Then, Peter Steinfels, professor of theology at Fordham University, preached on the Catholic Church's ongoing need for fresh talent to create new forms of worship and preaching, thereby attracting more souls into the fold. These highly trained graduates, seated before him, would make a difference, he said. Enthusiasm grew among his listeners. I remained unimpressed.

How I still bristled at this male-dominated world and its spiritual leadership of the Catholic world, relegating women to lesser roles. Old resentments assailed me. As a child, my gender prohibited me from serving Mass and from singing with the choir in our parish church. Sucked into voiceless passivity, I stormed, inwardly, for years. And before taking vows in the Society of the Sacred Heart, both in Albany, New York, and in Rome, I endured Canonical examinations by bishops' delegates; then knelt for their blessing; rituals, even then, I perceived as phony. And the November 1974 Latin form letter, number 56636/74, from the Sacra Congregatio Pro Religiosis Et Institutis Saecularibus dispensed me from perpetual vows in the Society. And still later, I greeted and handed Mass programs to worshippers streaming through the oak doors of St. Francis Xavier, the Jesuit parish I joined in 1976 upon my return to St. Louis. There, I also organized the ushers, lectored, and cleaned up after parish socials.

However, a blip in that dismal scenario occurred in 1982. I smiled. Yearning for more participation in the ministry, I began training as a chaplain through the Association of Clinical Pastoral Education at the St. Louis State Psychiatric Hospital. Our supervisor, Serge Castiglione, a Lutheran minister, styled himself as "bishop" of that facility and "ordained" us to full participation in the ministry. That included Sunday Mass in the basement chapel. There, I once experienced my priesthood, the words of consecration over the bread and wine, fire-flashing through my entire being. Later that same morning, I passed the basket for the collection at St. Francis Xavier.

Suddenly, everyone was standing for the creed, sung in full voice. The walls of the chapel swelled with pride, like a high-pitched accordion. Too much to deal with, I zoned out. After the jubilant "Amen," I sat down and arched my back against the pew, then massaged my sore knees. Dominican concelebrants carried the Mass forward within the established protocol, until the madness finally ended. It was time for graduation.

Mother sniffled as the registrar announced Mark's name, and the president of Aquinas Institute, the Dominican Charles Bouchard, handed him a leather-covered degree. All smiles, Mark stood tall among the applause, then returned to his pew among the graduates. Mother's tears prompted my offer of help.

"Not now. I can't talk about it," Mother snapped, hurriedly wiping her eyes and balling her handkerchief in her purse. And we never did. I was still an irritant to her, despite my Ninth Step amends, which she had coolly dismissed the last time we were together. Yet I still yearned to become a real daughter before she died, not just an appendage, and my morning AA meetings across the street continued deepening my understanding about relationships. In time, I hoped Mother would respond.

Finally it was over. Dominican professors surrounded Mark with congratulations, then opened their circle to admit Mother who hugged him, again tearfully. "I'm so proud of you, Mark!" she said, rubbing the back of her hand over her eyes. "You've done so well!"

I steamed. Again Mark was her favorite son.

There was more. "I never could have done this without your help," Mark said, tensing his clean-shaven face over Mother's shoulder, the red tassel on his mortarboard swinging. Then Mark showed her his degree, this followed by more hugs. All around me, other graduates beamed before cameras held by loved ones. The noise was deafening. I needed to leave, desperately, but I had to wait for Mother and Mark. I was their chauffeur to C. J. Whittaker's for an early supper.

That night, emotionally wrung out, I telephoned Ellen. Her bright voice reassured me. "Liz, you're in another dry drunk. You've no control over Mark and your mother. Let them be. Surrender your pride and rage to God. Let Him help you." I knew she was right. She knew me better than anyone I'd ever known. She had become my nurturing mother, responsive to my calls for help in between our weekly analysis.

Ivory Sundress,
June 4, 1995

It was Pentecost evening at The Seven Gables Inn in Clayton where Mother and I sat on the patio, munching breadsticks and waiting for the Caesar salads we'd ordered. She was in a mellow mood as she fingered an ice cube in her Dewar's scotch-on-the-rocks. I sipped ice water. Around us, patrons nursed bubbly wines under umbrella tables, breezes laced the flagstones with spent apple blossoms, and aromas from the kitchen whetted our appetites. Comfortable in my ivory sundress, I crossed my ankles, relieved of knee pain for a while, and studied Mother's flowered jacket and white slacks, accessorized with Mark's blue costume jewelry, now her favorite.

"That dress becomes you, Liz. Is it new?" Mother asked, twisting her diamond engagement ring on her finger. There was that question again. I shook my head, gripped my hands in my lap, then wiggled my toes in my red sandals.

Soft winds glanced off my freckled forehead, as I recalled my discovery, years before, of Seconds, a women's store featuring clothes that models had worn in shows around the country. "No," I said to Mother. "It's another dress from Seconds. I've worn it before—many times—I love its texture, its woven tie-belt." I must have looked lovely sitting across from Mother that evening, with my willowy neck, firm shoulders and upper arms toned by laps at the St. Louis University Rec Center pool. There, breast-strokes had expanded my lungs and momentarily enlarged my wellbeing, until I climbed out of the pool and limped toward the locker room.

"Liz, you've become a lovely woman," Mother abruptly added. Her eyes fixed on me, then dropped to her perspiring drink from which she took a sip. In that brief second, I glimpsed her heart, as I had that morning in the Kenwood parlor before receiving the novice's habit. Then, she had cried holding me in her arms, careful not to muss my Alcenon lace veil she had bought in Brussels the year before for the brides in her family. I was the first of many to wear it. Thereafter, mutual fears clamped shut our hearts.

But this evening was different. Mother experienced something different in me and felt compelled to say so. I lost my voice. Then again we retreated into our worlds. It was safer that way, despite my yearning to return to that warm place I'd glimpsed in hers. Thereafter, it haunted me.

At the next table sat another mother and daughter with an infant gumming her pacifier stretching chubby fingers to the sky as if to catch a stray apple blossom. For an instant, my childless condition stung, a feeling always evoked by mothers holding infants shining like suns. I ached for this intimacy. At best, elderly patients I'd been visiting for years in DePaul Hospital and later with Incarnate Word Home Care and Hospice welcomed me as their "caring daughter," shared stories on their front porches, around kitchen tables or bedrooms—life reviews that enlarged my world. Not so with my mother. I often wondered if we'd ever bonded after my breech birth that had plummeted her into toxic shock, an experience she breezily shared during one of our Sundays together.

Then our waitress approached our table, carrying salads, but they were not for us.

I munched another breadstick, looked at Mother fingering her beads. She had more to say. "Already you've the beginnings of a tan. Something I could never do with my fair skin. I've always had to watch my complexion, something my mother insisted upon." And there were others: designer gowns, freshly coiffed hair, catered dinner parties, surrounded by guests in formal attire. And still others: maintaining a "don't-touch" home where messes were outlawed; feigning polite silences rather than speaking up; living within the shadow of her spouse; bearing a child every two years—all influences stemming from the post-Victorian view of upper-class Catholic women who were to look pretty and not cause trouble.

Then our waitress placed our salads before us, asked Mother if she wanted a refill. She shook her head, unfolded her napkin on her lap, forked some greens, and chewed slowly, but not without hurriedly swiping a tear from her eye. Never in my fifty-nine years had I been so moved.

Silence accompanied our first mouthfuls of crisp greens, until Mother placed her fork on her plate, stretched back against the chair, and said, "Tell me about your Mass at St. Francis this morning. Was it as beautiful as other years?"

She'd often asked that question, an occasional check, in my perception, that I'd not rejoined Trinity Episcopal Church, that I'd not placed my immortal soul in jeopardy. It had been quite a scene that afternoon in 1991, when bone-tired of her concerns over my church attendance, I told her of my confirmation in the Episcopal Church.

Mother's excitement mounted as I described the morning's pageantry at St. Francis Xavier, done up in reds: wicker baskets of azaleas on the sanctuary floor, flaming candles upon bronze standards squaring the corners of the table altar, ribboned banners with symbols of Spirit, red-sashed dancers carrying pots of incense, celebrants in swishing vestments, mixed voices of the choir creating ethereal hymns—the Pentecost experience I had had in that church for many years. What she did not know was my rage after the choir's last "Amen," my tearing outside the great doors, and racing home to the quiet of my study. Indeed, this year's Pentecost later found its way into a poem I wrote, titled "The Good Ol' Boys Club."

Satisfied by my narration, Mother resumed eating, the shoulder pads in her jacket dwarfing her stooped frame. Her osteopenia was worsening.

Over decaffeinated coffee, we ended the evening reviewing preparations for my sister's second wedding in a few weeks, an event that would bring our extended family to Toledo, Ohio. I felt Mother's advice coming. "As matron of honor, you must have a new gown. Perhaps one evening after work we can shop. When can we meet?"

I held my ground, having already decided to wear my peach chiffon gown rather than buy something new.

That night, I tossed in bed, still overwhelmed by Mother's brilliant blue eyes affirming my loveliness, yet dashed by the look's disappearance. At the time, I thought something was wrong with me. Eventually, I fell asleep and woke later with this dream.

Elizabeth

I am traveling with Mother in an underground Scandinavian city. On both sides are women who have had multiple births. They appear exhausted, despondent. Then Mother wants to return to our hotel room for an enema to move her bowels before the day's end. I continue the tour with our guide. Twelve lightsome women approach us and reveal secrets of their inner beauty. Joy overwhelms me, despite my inability to remember what they said.

I woke deeply consoled, yet stunned by the visit of these "twelve lightsome women," their eagerness to share the mysteries of the Sacred Feminine. All my life, I had been hoodwinked by patriarchal theologies emanating from the twelve tribes of Israel found in the Jewish tradition, and later, the twelve apostles in the Christian tradition, as had my mother and her mother. Together, these theologies cast a womb-like world around me, peopled by the women in my extended family and the Sacred Heart nuns who had taught me at Villa Duchesne and Maryville College and later formed me as a nun at Kenwood. Such as it was back then. There was no chink in this constricted theology, supported for thousands of years by impressive temples and cathedrals all over the world. Only in such places could the Divine be accessed. It took years before I grasped the Sacred Feminine within me, but this dream foreshadowed its presence.

Interesting that twelve years later, 2007, I wrote to the pastor of St. Francis Xavier Church, requesting that my name be withdrawn from its rolls. It was time. That morning I had had this dream.

I'm in the vestibule of St. Francis Xavier Church sitting inside a miniature red car, similar to those driven by Shriners during their parades. Around me are many other cars manned by parishioners. We await the signal for the entrance procession and the beginning of Mass. A carnival air swells the entire church. The organ silences the mayhem, our signal to rev up our cars. Ahead of me, the cars move. Midway up the aisle, my car swerves out of line, accelerates ahead of the others, makes a sharp right turn in front of the sanctuary, and plows through the exit. Laughing, I bounce down the stone steps to sunshine, blue skies enlivening Lindell Boulevard.

I had found another way through the 12 Steps of Alcoholics Anonymous. There was no going back.

21

Lilly Pulitzer Orange-Gold Dress, Mother's Day, 1996

"Will all the mothers please remain standing for a special blessing?" the perspiring pastor asked at the end of Mass, celebrated at All Saints, Mark's parish in University City where he lived. Once a thriving complex established in 1921, only a handful of worshippers filled the pews in this octagonal church; above us, sunshine filtered through Emil Frei's stained glass windows, subtly executed in yellow and brown tones. I sat down, crossed my knees. Mother preened in her pink Bleyle suit and pearls, with white pumps and handbag, her rouged cheeks unusually flushed. She loved being honored by Holy Mother Church in this way, Mother's Day after Mother's Day. It had always been the same. The blessing droned on, toddlers squirming next to their mothers. After the "Amen!" Mark, now sporting a moustache, rushed from the choir, his baritone complementing other voices, and kissed Mother on both cheeks, then gave me a fleeting glimpse while cupping her elbow down the aisle toward the back of the church. There, ushers handed white carnations tied with pink ribbons to all the mothers.

Again I seethed. For decades, I had "mothered" the acutely ill and dying in hospitals or their inner city homes. None were lovely in pastels with freshly groomed hair; they were more often in faded robes and torn hairnets with bad breath. Nor had anyone recognized my efforts, save with paltry paychecks, much less present me with flowers. Resentments swamped me. I needed an AA meeting, but that was not possible until later.

Mother and Mark chatted during the drive to Greenbriar Hills Country Club for the Mother's Day brunch for our extended family, a ritual she had organized since the late 1970s. Occasionally I glimpsed their animation through my rear-view mirror, then studied flowering quince trees lining the highway.

In mincing tones, Mother said, "Mark, tell me more about your work at Raven last week. Since you became director, you keep making changes."

Again I glanced at Mother, her blue eyes alive with interest, anticipating his response. Mark seemed to have found his niche in this counseling center addressing male battering. He stood taller, a new liveliness in his speech and movements. His revamping the program had attracted more participants in the therapy groups. Additional funding helped spruce up the center, then located in a walk-up above the Ferrari Consignment Shop at 7314 Manchester Road in Maplewood.

"A lot's been going on," Mark added, obviously pleased she had asked. "Again, I've been invited to speak at several boys' high schools. It appalls me how little is known about this age-old problem. It starts young." He paused, loosened his tie, then asked, "Liz, will you please turn on the air conditioner? It's a little warm back here."

Elizabeth

More chatter destabilized me, causing me to miss the turnoff onto Big Bend and the Greenbriar Hills Country Club. Mother grimaced. This would delay her arrival. As hostess, she always liked to arrive before her guests to wish them a Happy Mother's Day. Mark became strangely quiet seeing Mother's ill-temper. Still flummoxed, I later dropped them off at the entrance of the club, banked with formal beds of pansies and dusty miller, then parked near greening lawns adjacent to the golf course. Already crowds of families had arrived.

Earlier, I squirmed under Mother's long look at my Lilly Pulitzer orange-gold dress—one I could afford, thanks to my inheritance, years before, from Dad's estate. Too form-revealing, I sensed, according to tastes she'd internalized from her mother. On her thirteenth birthday, Grandmother had put her into a corset, seen as an initiatory rite into young womanhood. There was no discussion. Her friends also blandly accepted this rite, even became dependent upon zippers mashing unseemly bulges beneath "little black jersey dresses," popularized by the French designer Coco Chanel. Whirls of tea parties, cotillions at the St. Louis Women's Club, summer dances at Norwood Hills Country Club, the Veiled Prophet's Ball, debutante gowns and later wedding gowns kept dressmakers busy. Make-up and bobbed hair kinked by permanents augmented the post-Victorian women, who revealed arms, shoulders, backs, and calves for the first time. It was a wild time, juiced with alcohol, cigarettes, dancing the Charleston in speakeasies on Delmar Boulevard, but only on the surface. Once home, Mother and her peers fell within the invisible restraints of Church and family, powerless to escape. Such was my impression from Mother's stories over the years. The drudgery of keeping house for her growing children, despite maids, laundresses, and cooks lightening the burden, was never mentioned. Yet the 1920s partying was still replicated in the elegant homes of her friends.

Inside our private dining room, I found Mark at Mother's elbow, scrupulously attending to her needs lest she be in want of anything. My siblings and their spouses, in high spirits, encircled them. At the long banquet table, decorated with bowls of pink and white tulips and flaming candles in hurricane lamps, sat married nieces and nephews in clusters; their children zoomed in and out of the room in stockinged feet, their rumpled party dresses and shirt tails flying after them. We were now twenty-eight with a twenty-ninth soon to be born. Waitresses in white uniforms trimmed in black, their black aprons trimmed in white, circulated Bloody Marys and wine and Cokes. One served me a glass of ice water I slowly nursed.

Assuming my loving-aunt persona, I received hugs from the younger set and joined them. The St. Louis Cardinals' loss to the Los Angeles Dodgers, the night before, drew varied comments, in between recipes and childrearing tips. Quickly, I was at sea, although still smiling. Checking my watch, I longed for the moment we could move into the dining room, its buffet tables stacked with enticing foods—anything to assuage my multiple hungers.

While waiting, I walked out to the brick patio and mulled over the morning's dream; it still horrified me.

I'm a senior at Maryville College in south St. Louis, my present age and circumstances, still struggling with a philosophy course required for graduation. One of my peers, wanting to keep a pet in her room, finds a blackbird and intends to break its wildness.

Curiosity draws nearby students; their merriment escalates, as they watch her tie a cord around the bird's neck, then release it onto the floor. Frenzied, it appears distressed as it writhes about, unable to escape its torturer. The bird's luster fades; its feathers become matted, broken, dull. Everyone shrieks with laughter, until the bird, exhausted, topples over and dies. I feel very bad, but do nothing.

Questions unnerved me. Who was that student with a killer instinct? No one I knew. What influences from the core curriculum, from the world surrounding us, had led her to such a dastardly act, those same influences that had also formed my passivity in the dream, my passivity in real life, as if sleepwalking with my eyes wide open? Perhaps I myself was that student, effectively killing my instinctual life through poor choices. Like attending this family gathering that was further depleting my vital energies. The truth seared. In my orange-gold dress, I felt like the blackbird, slowly losing its soul.

Then a gong sounded. It was the headwaiter summoning us to the buffet tables before they were cleared away. Drinks in hand, everyone hurried into the dining room. It was finally time to eat.

Atop the central buffet table, a profusion of tulips, irises, and roses surrounded an ice sculpture of a pelican, its melting caught in a green drape around its base. Another bird was dying, aquatic this time, slowly, drip-by-drip. No one seemed to notice. Of more importance were bronze warmers with placards in front of each, makings for fresh omelets and Belgian waffles, rounds of cheeses and crackers from distant lands, baskets and trays of sweet rolls, bowls of fresh fruit, salads, platters of pastries. Weary uniformed servers perked up to accommodate our needs.

Lilly Pulitzer Orange-Gold Dress, Mother's Day, 1996

Mother fingered her pearls, frowned over the picked-over remnants of elegant foods in the warmers. She was paying for our meal.

As Mark handed her a plate, she said, "There's not much left. It's happened again. We're late. We've spent too much time talking." After serving herself some asparagus and eggs Benedict, she moved toward the salad table.

Mark followed, placating her mood. "Look, Mother, there's still a large selection. Even fresh shrimp," he said patting her shoulder. "You like that. Let me serve you. And perhaps some of this pasta salad over here with the sundried tomatoes." Filling another plate, he offered it to her.

Satisfied, Mother lingered while Mark filled his plate. Always a big eater, he sampled everything, often taking seconds. Then I followed them to our dining room, where others were already engrossed in their food. Little conversation. Still others joined us for more serious eating until our table was filled. More drink orders were taken, amidst discussion of handicaps for the afternoon's golf game.

With second cups of coffee, ribboned gifts appeared before the mothers around the table. I watched. With others, I clucked over this or that blouse, sweater, purse, circulated the Mother's Day greeting cards around the table, touched that my goddaughter had remembered me. More exclamations filled this ritual, verging on monotony. Suddenly, shrieks—they seemed to come from beneath the table—then pounding fists, kicking feet. Everyone stood, looked aghast. Within the folds of the banquet cloth was two-year-old Colleen on her stomach, her sundress in tangles, her make-believe tears transformed into giggles. Laughter rose to the timbered ceiling. I laughed as well, the outburst releasing my tension. Mark calmed Mother, who again was fingering her pearls. The whole afternoon had been a comic performance that went flat. On some level, everyone knew it, but in Mother's presence would never admit it, least of all Mark. More than ever, their bond appeared seamless: her eighty-seven years of mothering, his forty-five years of financial dependence.

Like cumulative sands in an hourglass, I slowly woke to my tenuous position in the family. Shame and guilt, long buried in the unconscious, had mandated looking good, especially in settings like Greenbriar Hills Country Club. On some level, I went along with this, muffling passions beneath bland exchanges that passed for conversation. But unlike the blackbird in my dream, I knew I would not die. Unlike the blackbird, "habited" in black, I loved my Lilly Pulitzer orange-gold dress and would continue showing off my willowy body, a subtle way of rebelling against Mother. Still more dreams prodded me toward actualizing my gift as woman, but there still would be more years of Sundays with Mother. She was like a drug I was not free to discard. Beneath her styled white hair lurked rage, corseted in perfectionism. She could still hurt me if I disappointed her. Perhaps Mark felt the same way.

22

Striped Wool Pullover, April 1998

"Liz, this just came in the mail. Immediately I thought of you," Ellen exclaimed, waving a brochure as I arrived for my Friday hour, balancing my dream book together with books she had loaned me. Her penchant was to draw her analysands into explorations of their own unconscious, rather than spoon-feed them. However because of anxiety related to arthritic pain, I only skimmed opening chapters of books she shared or recommended I buy. Evidently, that was enough, because there was no dearth of dreams. Morning after morning, they woke me.

"Come into my study and I'll tell you more," Ellen exclaimed, her round face beaming, a silk scarf with gold tones complementing her sweater. Following her recommendations, in previous years I had joined tours by Jungian guides to sites of the Sacred Feminine in Italy, Egypt, and Ireland, despite great difficulty walking. For each tour, I had worn my striped wool pullover, a gift from Mother many years before. I sensed another tour coming.

"This one is to Greece," she said, as she handed me the brochure, then set her writing board on her lap for our hour. Incense perfumed her study, filled with bookcases, figurines and masks from her world travels, mementoes from other analysands, potted plants greening before tall windows. Correspondence and abstracts littered her desk and worktable. Her dog Max was in the kitchen. "Eleanora Wolloy and her daughter Susanna Brown, both from Virginia Beach, will co-lead a small group of women," Ellen added, putting on her glasses and grabbing a pen. "They're leaving at the end of March. You might consider joining them."

As it was pointless to protest the insufficient time to study for such a trip, I tucked the brochure into my dream book and prepared for our hour. There it stayed for weeks. Ellen did not bring up it up during subsequent hours.

Then a nightmare jarred me.

I am invited to participate in a ritual. I have nothing suitable to wear. A friend loans me a beautiful black silk gown with a fitted bodice, billowing skirt. It looks stunning. I meet a handsome red-haired man who kneels before me, places his large hands on my hips, presses his head upon my womb, and prays for the offspring. Then he leaves...On my way to return the gown to my friend, two pythons slither toward me, one ahead of the other. I'm terrified. I fall and cannot get up. One of the pythons approaches my head. I'm going to be bitten.

Still shuddering, I retrieved the brochure from my dream book and studied the itinerary; its pace exhausted me. After landing in Athens, a bus, plane, or boat would transport the participants to seven different hotels within eleven days to explore ancient sanctuaries of the Goddess. Eleusis, outside Athens, was one of them. That struck a chord from Robert Graves's *The Greek Myths*, one of the books Ellen had recommended I own. An initiation rite into the mysteries of dying and rebirth had been celebrated there, one honoring the Demeter-Persephone myth, found in the Homeric Hymns dating back to the seventh century B.C. Later classical writers, Ovid and Aristophanes, also recorded this myth as it continued evolving in oral tradition. All of this gave me pause. Then I scribbled the nightmare in my dream book; it also suggested an initiation rite, one I was not free to disregard. I was about to be bitten.

During my next hour with Ellen, she corroborated my impressions of the nightmare, especially its initiatory character, and supported my decision to join the tour to Greece. "There, you'll discover more significance, critical to your becoming woman," she said, smiling, fingering a coral pendant she wore around her neck.

"You're going to Greece?" Mother asked during a phone call after I'd secured time off from work. From the tone in her voice, I imagined frown lines deepening her brow, her fingers twisting the cord on the receiver next to her desk in the family room. "It'll be a rough trip," she added. "Probably too much for you, especially given your back problems last month." I cringed, again remembering how sciatic pain had destabilized me in 1982, and how she had taken me into her home for four weeks. Her eighty-nine years now precluded such care.

"No need to worry, Mother," I said. "You know how well I got along on other tours." Of my severe bronchitis in Egypt, my painful knees in Ireland, I'd said nothing. There was critical learning in Greece, and I had to avail myself of it.

However, with my deepening enthusiasm, Mother's attitude changed. A world traveler herself, she began sharing experiences of her Aegean cruise with Dad and Mark, many years before. Of particular note was a donkey ride, up some mountain pass, that had left her sore. Lost to her were the symbolic meanings of marble and stone remnants of temples, enshrined in museums, strewn upon wide plains. After all, the Greek gods and goddesses were pagan. I too held this view while teaching mythology to ninth graders at Villa Duchesne; its sole intent was to explain classical allusions found in English literature they would later study.

The chilly morning of my departure, Mother insisted taking me in a cab to the airport. Beneath her navy beret, her eyes were moist as she kissed me goodbye and pressed a wad of bills into my hand. "Get something for yourself," she said, waving me off.

During the flight to JFK, I again flipped through the pages of Graves's book, mulled over the Demeter-Persephone myth. Breathless, I reentered the story of this mother and her fair daughter, both earth goddesses, joyous in each other's presence. One afternoon while picking poppies in a meadow, Persephone was unaware of the earth opening behind her. It was Hades, god of the underworld in his horse-drawn chariot; enamored by her youth, he grabbed her, thrust her next to him, then reversed his black steeds for their reentry into the underworld. All the while, Persephone yelled, "Rape! Rape!" The crone goddess, Hecate, witnessed this abduction and informed Demeter.

Striped Wool Pullover, April 1998

Outraged, Demeter immediately set out to find her daughter, but to no avail. So distraught was she, the earth began to wither and die. To remedy this intolerable situation, Zeus, father of the gods, sent another god to persuade Hades to relinquish his bride to her mother. He did so, but not before she had eaten seven seeds of the pomegranate, and assured him of her return three months of each year. Eleusis was reputed to be the site of this mother-daughter reunion.

Years later, this curious myth about a necessary loss, a necessary search, and a reunion would become central in mine.

Blankly, I stared at cloud stacks miles below the plane, until again stirred by the image of the pomegranate in the myth—symbol of the woman's womb with its fructifying seeds. I breathed deeply, remembering my initiatory dream that had prompted this tour. Had that red-haired man seeded me? Why? Perhaps in time, I would learn. I had to be patient. Then the book fell from my hands as I nodded off to sleep.

Later, I found my way into the International Terminal, pulling my suitcase behind me. In the distance stood a woman with long red hair framing her oval face, carrying a placard with the name of our tour. Her fragile beauty enhanced by the soft beige tones of her attire stunned me. Around her rushed other travelers heading toward the escalators. Immediately, I threaded my way toward her.

"Hi! I'm Liz Moloney from St. Louis," I said, surprised by the strength in my voice. Her brown eyes warmed me.

"Great to meet you, Liz! I'm Susanna Brown," she said in resonant tones. "Here's an envelope with your plane tickets and other helpful information. Check in with Olympia Airlines, and then join Mother and some of the other women in the lounge upstairs. I'll catch up with you after I meet the others." Reassured by her smile, I walked with more confidence.

"So you're Liz! Welcome!" A matronly woman with highlighted blonde hair tied in a bun opened her arms. It was Eleanora, a flowered shawl caught in her elbows. "Ellen told me you were coming. I so enjoy seeing her during our Inter-Regional meetings. She's so wise, so generous. Come. Let me introduce you to the others." A blur of names and greetings followed. I found a place on the sofa and listened. Like myself, many were in analysis. Quickly, we bonded with Eleanora, whose lithesomeness bespoke the feminine. Tapered fingers set off designer rings; gold bangles, on her wrist. Among such seasoned women, colorfully dressed and with intriguing jewelry, I was sure to learn much. This had been true of other Jungian tours.

My expectation mounted during the ocean crossing seated between Ann from Carbondale, Illinois, with her Evil-Eye bracelet she had bought during a trip to Turkey, and Peggy from Virginia Beach, Virginia. Upon touchdown in Athens, I joined in the passengers' spontaneous applause.

After checking into the Palace Electra Hotel located in the Plaka area of Athens, I settled in and rested until our evening orientation in a red-draped conference room. Anticipation mounted as I joined the others already seated in a circle of twenty-three chairs; on each, a white candle. At the head sat Eleanora and Susanna, both changed into flowing wool dresses, complementary shawls, and pumps.

Striped Wool Pullover, April 1998

Eleanora's ringed fingers rested upon a notepad as she said, "A warm welcome to each of you! We hope your rooms are comfortable, that you're warm enough. Who would have believed yesterday's snowfall—here in Athens? A good omen for us," she said. Everyone stirred in their chairs, some smiling, some wiping sleep from their eyes. "The next ten days will be very full," she added. "You've noted, midway, we've planned a break on the island of Mykonos, a curious world of white stucco houses with blue trim. Some even have tiny chapels." Then she enumerated the sacred sites we would visit: the Acropolis in Athens, Epidaurus, Olympia, Delphi, the island of Delos, Crete, lastly Eleusis. Everyone sensed the ordeal ahead.

"Aside from the history enshrining these ancient sites, their marble and stone remnants scattered by earthquakes over the centuries—we'll also have a native guide accompanying us— we want to pay close attention to our interior landscapes, our dreams, fantasies, our hunches. Our intent is to open ourselves to the voice of the Sacred Feminine among us, to hear her affirming voice.

"As you've surmised, this will be an arduous initiation for each of us. Each evening after supper we'll meet and review the day's experiences, offer support to each other." Strong feeling filled the room as she spoke.

Then Eleanora paused, a glimmer of a smile on her lips, a loose strand of blonde hair feathering her forehead. "Those from Virginia Beach who've traveled with us would appreciate knowing the others. Perhaps this'd be a good time to share backgrounds, expectations, that sort of thing, what brought you here." Everyone nodded. "Then my daughter and I will begin."

Elizabeth

I listened intently, one woman's story more impressive than the next. Among them were artists of every stripe: counselors in private practice, entrepreneurs, retired professionals, mothers, and grandmothers, women reflecting the authority of the Women's Movement I had only brushed against because of chronic fatigue. Many hailed from the Southeast; one from Texas fashioned jewelry from semi-precious stones.

Then, it was my turn. Standing at my place, my words coming slowly, I spoke. "My name is Liz Moloney, from St. Louis. My analyst, Ellen Scheire, recommended I join this tour. I've been on similar tours to sacred shrines, but the Feminine Mysteries still elude me. Perhaps it will be different this time." I paused and looked around the circle. Smiles, everywhere, just like those around the tables of Alcoholics Anonymous. I concluded, "At home, I work as a hospice chaplain, helping terminally ill patients transition to the next life and supporting their loved ones." Tingling, I sat down and fidgeted with my candle. This just might work.

After the last woman's comments, Eleanora and Susanna lowered the lights, lit their candles, then passed their flames to each of us. Faces glowed in the shadows anticipating the close of the fiery circle. Then silence—we were one in the fire. In solemn tones, Eleanora began a prayer to the Sacred Feminine encapsulating all the Goddesses. I yearned to be open to Her whisperings, still foreign to me.

Later that evening we trekked to a noisy taverna filled with singing and dancing patrons, Eleanora at my elbow answering my questions. Everything looked strange, especially five-thousand-year-old buildings we passed, shrouded with heavy canvas; too valuable to tear down, they awaited investors to restore them or archaeological teams to explore their riches.

Striped Wool Pullover, April 1998

The next morning I awoke from a telling dream.

I continue cleaning my home in preparation for my teacher, a beautiful man.

Eleanora smiled when I shared it with her over breakfast. "Continue listening," she said. "There's much to learn here. Even for us who've been here several times."

Our first sacred site was the Parthenon, a Doric temple honoring Pallas Athena, atop the Acropolis in Athens. Despite freezing winds and threatening skies, Soho, our guide, led our ascent up slick marble steps to the Propylaia, or entrance with five porticos. In the distance loomed the Erechtheum with the Caryatids, six maidens of unsurpassing beauty, and still farther, the Parthenon shrouded in greys. Suddenly gusts of wind slammed into me. I crouched, then inched my way over to the guardrails and held on with all my strength. I could move no farther. Helen, a retired nurse, noted my terror and grabbed on to me. Together, we made our descent to our heated bus. Others from our tour, silenced by their ordeal, were warming themselves.

The following days, we visited Epidaurus, place of Aesclepian healing to which I brought my arthritic body, my gift of hospice care. Invigorated by the chilly pine-scented air, I breathed deeply, a new freedom coursing through my body. Later bussed to Olympia, the mountain dwelling of the gods and goddesses and, for centuries, the site of athletic competitions, I was challenged to continue exercising, despite fiery joints. And at Delphi, the ruins of Apollo's Temple built over the prehistoric shrine of the Earth Goddess, Gaia, and her pythons, I again experienced their terrifying slithering, as in that dream that had compelled me to join this tour. Despite exhaustion, I was afire.

That evening after supper in the Amalia Delphi Hotel, Eleanora suggested my horror of the pythons was consistent with the initiation experience, as well those terrifying moments atop the Acropolis. I had only to surrender to the process. It was underway. On sofas around me, other women listened, wide-eyed, then shared their impressions of Gaia. Among them, I caught vague murmurings of the Sacred Feminine, strong, gentle.

The following days, we traveled to Mykonos, to Delos, then on to Crete, then back to the outskirts of Athens and the shrine at Eleusis, our last stop. Again sitting next to me on our bus was Eleanora, a paisley silk scarf draped over her shoulder. Her eyes warmed as she said, "Liz, your work as a hospice chaplain must have acquainted you with the mysteries of dying and rebirth. Fits in with where we're going."

"Yes," I said, "I've learned much from our patients and their families, especially how to handle my own dying, a surrender like none other. But it's the little ones that keep me stymied, like my reluctance to join this tour—with my knees and all. I'm surprised I'm doing as well as I am. Ann's been a big help." Often she was at my elbow, steadying my steps along rocky paths, climbing hills, getting off the bus.

"I've noticed that, Liz. Everyone's glad you made the tour. Your sharing in the evening has opened others to deeper truth about themselves. As women, we've a richness few have actualized. Our culture is rife with pitfalls, with messages of women's insignificance. As you've experienced, the intent of this tour is to counter such negativity with images of Goddesses enshrined in what remains of their temples. Each day nudges us toward unexplored realms within our psyches. Yours is quite rich—you're responding well to the inner teacher in the dream you shared with me that first morning over breakfast."

Two days before our flight home, I shivered in my striped wool pullover, picking my way among toppled marble columns and tympanums. This was Eleusis. In the distance, cypresses lined the hills against a china-blue sky, obscuring the industrial area surrounding us. My companions took off across a level area of paving stones, leaving me alone. I wanted it that way. With my knees beginning to buckle, I leaned against a mottled grey rock, despite it being prohibited. In front of me, gentle winds swayed a solitary full-blown poppy. Within its red-orange aura, I again pieced together the myth of Demeter and Persephone, how their initiates, over the centuries, had streamed along the Sacred Way from Athens to this site, anticipating rebirth, just as we had. Imperceptibly, I awoke to old attitudes and behaviors that still kept me fearful and restricted my breathing. An urgency demanded life above ground, in the sunshine, in the bracing air.

Aware of other areas to explore, I headed toward the Well of the Beautiful Women, purported to be the site where Demeter, exhausted from her search for Persephone, had rested. A circle of marble stones petalled its opening; inside, dusty cobwebs, soot. Because nothing moved me here, I limped toward the Plutonium, the half-moon cave on the distant hill, where Persephone had been restored to her mother. Suddenly, a dark force crimped my breathing. Lest I fall, I lowered myself onto a rock a few steps behind me.

Like Persephone before her return to her mother, I was silent, dumb, captive to an alien foe that kept me drained of vital energy, a lethargy I was powerless to escape. Despite momentary glimpses of freedom during analysis with Ellen, in dreams, around the tables of Alcoholics Anonymous, in the gaiety of Eleanora and Susanna and the other women, I glimpsed my continuing enmeshment in Mother's elegant world, filled with subtle negative energy. I could see that now, despite efforts to disentangle from her and become my own woman. More frustration burned when I remembered her anxious eyes when we had parted at the airport.

Leaving the poppy behind, I inched closer toward the yawning cave, then strained my eyes into its darkness that mirrored my own. Suddenly, laughter rained down from above. I looked up into the sun; framed against it were my new friends who had scaled the hill. I blinked hard, envious of their vitality. Mine was spent.

Before flying out of Athens, our tour stopped at a specialty store. I had sent a raft of postcards to family and friends, picked out a replica of the Minoan Snake Goddess for Ellen, but had not bought anything for myself. On one of the walls, a board painting of Demeter holding sheaves of wheat and poppies in upright hands, a gesture of prayer, stopped me in my tracks. Her eyes invited communion, a way of actualizing my birthright. I teared up, knowing I had been visited. However, still tenuously involved in Roman Catholic theology, I moved toward other wares. A display case of icons next caught my attention. Among them was an Annunciation, the angel Gabriel impregnating the Virgin Mary. My heart soared. Again that pre-tour dream flashed before me, the kneeling red-haired man, a priest figure, his hands embracing my hips, his head bowed into my abdomen, praying for the offspring within. This was it. I had been impregnated anew. It would be birthed, somehow. I burned.

Striped Wool Pullover, April 1998

I bought the three-hundred-dollar icon with some of Mother's gift money. It still hangs in my study and I kiss it, often.

More years of dream analysis would pass, as well as Mother's debilitating stroke and death, before I could allow "the pythons" in that dream to bite me with their gifts.

23

Enameled Heart Brooch,
April 18, 2000

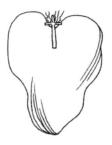

"I've another brochure, Liz," Ellen said, as I settled into her over-stuffed leather chair, opposite hers, for another hour. She had that look in her eye. There would be another trip. "You remember Clarissa Pinkola Estés and her book, *Women Who Run with the Wolves*?" she asked, handing me the brochure. "She'll be speaking at the New Harmony Inn in New Harmony, Indiana. It's next month. You might want to take it in. And you won't have to cross an ocean to get there, just a few hours' drive from St. Louis," she added, brushing a strand of blonde hair from her eyes. She was wearing a silver ring with a dark stone I'd not seen before.

Indeed I did remember that book I had bought in 1993; its vision of the wild woman archetype, identified with female wolves, had stoked my wildness, fired my darkness, seared my lethargy. A lifelong receiver of stories from around the world, Clarissa patterned them around her thesis: accessing Womanpower and surrendering to Her sure-footed guidance. For brief moments, lava ravished the core of my being. The burning was exquisite. Then I had to shelve the book in my study, where it remained among other Jungian books Ellen had recommended over the years. Other concerns kept me anxious and unable to concentrate: diminishing hospice referrals, because Tenet Healthcare Corporation had acquired our hospital; the breakdown of my left total knee replacement, now twenty-four years old; and Mother's ninety years and worsening heart condition. Still fired by Clarissa's vision, however, I'd occasionally leaf through a chapter in later years, again experience the burning and hear my cry, "If only if I could—then maybe—" until plunged into darkness, imaged, in retrospect, by the cave at Eleusis in Greece.

I had no choice but to attend Clarissa's lectures.

The dining room at the New Harmony Inn throbbed with expectation. Others had been captivated by Clarissa's vision and wanted to sit close to her fire, as I hoped to do. For her first talk, I expressly wore my ivory embroidered sweater atop my orange rayon skirt printed with small natives weaving gold and turquoise streamers. My wildness burned, while toying with the chicken entrée on my plate, listening to animated conversations around me, studying the tea lights burning around the centerpiece.

Finally it was time. The overhead fixtures dimmed. Applause followed Clarissa toward the lectern. A short, squat woman wearing a black silk floor-length gown, a black lace shawl limp in her elbows, she reached for the microphone, her dark eyes inviting her listeners into her story-world. Thick shoulder-length hair gave her a wild-woman appearance. Even more disconcerting was an enameled brooch of a flaming heart, similar to the one on my profession cross, pinned above her bosom.

Instantly, I was elsewhere, sitting on the motherhouse roof of the Society of the Sacred Heart in Rome, Italy. It was July 1965, a hot and humid evening. I was alone, my black habit saturated with perspiration. Sheltered by overhanging eaves, I mulled over the prescribed text for my meditation from the Gospel of St. John.

I heard the disciples of Jesus ask, "Who are you?" I, too, wanted to know, desperately, as I was preparing for final profession in the Society. He responded, "Come and see."

With that, the sky, a confluence of golds and blues and pinks, split apart and engulfed me in ethereal rhythms, a sweet burning. It felt as if I were inside the heart of God, and I did not want to leave. Ever. It was similar to those blinding Light moments the morning of my First Holy Communion, and others directing me toward the noviceship of the Society of the Sacred Heart and, later, marriage with Joe.

I shuddered, blinked hard, mesmerized by another heart, an enameled one heaving upon Clarissa's chest. Stroking it, she said in solemn tones, "This protects me whenever I'm in public." Then she seeded us with story after story. I burned listening to her. Like that evening on the motherhouse roof in Rome, I did not want to leave. But this was a different kind of burning—the dross of patriarchal attitudes and behaviors, imposed by the Catholic Church, my family, and the health system in which I worked—my entire world view, my self-understanding. I yearned for deeper initiation into the mystery of who I was. Clarissa assured us this same Power expanding our hearts this night would help us stay in the fire, to tend these seeds until they burst forth into new life.

Then followed comments and questions from the audience, primarily women, their energies like undulating waves wafting my spirit. I needed to be alone. I sipped ice water, my notebook still opened on my lap. With the last questioner satisfied, Clarissa concluded, "To weep is to remember who we really are and to submit to the new depth, some place in the future that is not yet." Then, with a mysterious smile, she wished us good night.

I tore outside into the dark and followed lighted brick paths to my room. Its simple furnishings in earth tones, hooked rugs, hardwood floors, warmed me, unlike the elegance of my condo in the Lindell Terrace, still reflecting Mother's tastes. Here I could breathe.

I collapsed on the bed, hugged my chest, its fires raging. Clarissa had challenged me to keep my heart open to this new fire, but could I stand it? It was a long wait until tomorrow's lecture. Sleep came in fits and starts, but I did have a curious dream, in retrospect, another seed.

...a mousy colorless woman reads from her life story, the dissertation written for her Jungian examiners. I'm astounded. One of her examiners joins us.

The "mousy colorless woman," her exterior belying her writerly gifts, gave me pause. She had a story that must be told. For this, she sought guidance from her Jungian mentors. I saw myself in this mousy and colorless woman, despite my fastidious grooming and attire, but, unlike her, saw little value in my life story. For years, Ellen had countered this perception and urged me to write about my convent experiences. Tired of her goading, I did complete a rough draft in 1996; it had felt like automatic writing. After my retirement, I was supposed to rework the draft into a memoir. However, I held on to my chaplain position, unconvinced I could ever learn to be a writer.

While I was styling my hair before the mirror, last night's image of black-gowned Clarissa with her gypsy eyes spirited me into this new day. My own Mother seemed anemic, her convoluted heart aggravated by aging and medications. Dismissing her from my thoughts, I headed toward the dining room that warm April morning. Perhaps after breakfast, a stroll around New Harmony would ground me. I knew I was in an historic place, established by George Rapp in 1814, envisioned as a refuge for his Christian theosophical and pietism movement begun in Iptingen, Germany, in 1804. That had been my practice visiting new cities, despite knee stiffness and low energy.

One of the sites I wanted to see was the Paul Tillich Park on North Main Street across from the Roofless Church, but I did not get there. Stabbing shin pain forced my return to my room to await lunch and Clarissa's lecture. I was scared, so far from home and from my orthopedic surgeon, not knowing anyone here. But I would stay. Clarissa had more to share.

That afternoon, we met Clarissa on the upper level of the Rapp-Owen Granary, a limestone, brick, and wood building dating to 1843, now used for conferences and weddings. Jammed within the small space, I sat with others eager for more feeding from this remarkable woman. We were not disappointed. This time, she wore a long musky-green dress that fell gracefully over her full figure, and matching green hose and black pumps; on her bosom, the heart brooch that fascinated me. Like the cacti, its root system fashioned to capture any moisture, the image with which she opened last night's lecture, I felt my soul moistened with vital energies. I would learn to live as woman, regardless of my past.

"The Mystical Rose," the title of this presentation, recalled one of the appellations in the Catholic litany of the Mother of Jesus; it recalled, as well, Dante's *Paradiso* in which a petalled white rose held the blessed, triumphant in new grace. I was yet to learn another meaning of this metaphor, one that still deepens with each entry into prayer.

Again without notes, seated on a straight-backed chair, Clarissa spoke of "The Mystical Rose," a feminine metaphor for the soul's fragrance. Again, I studied her fiery eyes with their challenge, the precision with which she articulated each word, the vital soul feeding that drew me deeper into the fire. My pen fell into my opened notebook in my lap. Awe precluded capturing her words, but I did scribble her closing remark, "Remember the essence. We can't live without it." Then the epiphany was over, and with hundreds of others, I descended the wooden steps, gripping the banister, and moved into the late afternoon sun. There would be more that evening.

Then behind me, a voice called, "Hi, aren't you Liz Moloney? From the Isis tour to Egypt four years ago?" I turned around. It was the woman who had used healing touch to break up my coughing spasm, while we had been returning to Luxor from the Temple of Isis/Hathor in Dendura. She looked stunning in her loose flowing dress, sandals, and beads that draped her full bosom, the afternoon sun glancing off her long brunette hair.

Still absorbed by Clarissa's remarks, I faltered, unable to recall her name. "Yes, it's good to see you again. That tour was exceptional, thanks to our guide."

"And the other women on the tour," she said. "Remember our initiation into the Isis mysteries our last evening together? At the Cairo Sheraton? I'm experiencing the same fire this weekend as I did back then."

My heart had burned as well. Dressed in my purple wool dress and gold jewelry, I stood barefoot with the others, awaiting my turn to move into the draped conference room. Inside were Nancy Qualls-Corbett and Wynette Barton, Jungian analysts from Birmingham, Alabama, and Austin, Texas, who had organized this tour. With raised arms, they intoned sacred words; then led me to the flaming brazier that consumed my blocks to the Sacred Feminine; then invited me to withdraw a marble egg, symbolizing new birth, from a pouch; then placed a silver medal of the Goddess Isis over my head; and then hugged me. It was a thrilling experience, enlarged during the lavish banquet that followed. However, the exhausting flight home and the return to Mother's world had eclipsed that experience.

Needing to be alone, I smiled, nodded to her, then headed toward my room.

Still mesmerized by Clarissa's enameled heart, I sat in the front row for her next presentation, "Participation Mystique as Restoration of Quintessential Sanity." Again waves of womb-warmth soothed my fire as she wove her spell among us. Steeped in more images, I held on for dear life, my pen limp in my hands. Then Clarissa paused, scrutinized her audience, and proclaimed, "Listen to the truth and it will make you strong, instead of cringing in fear." Morning after morning, I had heard this imperative around the tables of AA. It spoke of vibrant life, untrammeled by fears of displeasing Mother, my supervisors at work, and the Catholic Church. I longed for release through deeper practice of the Twelve Steps, but it had not come. At the time, I failed to understand that I needed a new God. Perhaps this was the gist of Clarissa's remarks.

Enameled Heart Brooch, April 18, 2000

Alone in my room again, cut off from the nurturing milieu, I lounged upon pillows stacked at the headboard, my notes and dream book at my side. I could not write. Everything hurt, especially my heart, a dried-up arroyo, an image internalized from Clarissa's presentations. Hugging a throw pillow, as I'd often seen new cardiac transplant patients do, I shut my eyes, lowered my head. Thready breathing disconcerted me. I was lost.

Suddenly the gloom lifted and my inner world was engulfed in flames. I was inside another heart that sought entrance into mine, felt the forced feeding of vital fluids. Terrible was the tension. I could not escape. Then the gloom returned.

Stunned, I slowly opened my eyes. It was midnight. I'd been visited, but by whom, by what? Sleep came instantly.

Sunday morning, I breakfasted alone, glad to be free of Mother, who, I assumed, had found a way to Mass. Then over to the Rapp-Owen Granary and Clarissa's last lecture, "The Use of Dreams to Mediate Envy, Loss of Meaning, and the Wandering Soul and Spirit." Again she wore her enameled brooch, this time affixed to a lavender dress that gave her a regal look. Again her motherly eyes pulled her listeners into her world, her ringed fingers stroking her brooch. She had promised that first evening to remain with us in the fire, and to it, I had to return. So did everyone else.

Clarissa began, her deep tones filling the Granary. It was uncanny, as if she were privy to last night's strange experience in my room. Her remarks seemed addressed only to me: the poisons of envy, of ennui, of restlessness killing the soul, and the imperative that these be addressed if change was to occur. For that, humility and honesty were critical. That was what remaining in the fire was all about. Suddenly, I felt pulled apart, lost my footing.

She was describing my soul's chaos mirrored in my dreams most mornings. But I lacked the heart to go beyond recording them in my notebook; some I reviewed with Ellen during analysis, but afterwards, had no recall of what we had shared. However, their testimony, since 1988, remains in notebooks, lined on shelves in my study.

Then it was over. Thunderous applause filled the Granary as Clarissa smiled, bowed, stroking her enameled heart, then took her leave among close friends. Stunned, I slowly followed the others down the wooden steps into the late morning sun. It also occurred to me that I'd missed Sunday Mass, a first for me. Instead of that predictable ritual which numbed me, I'd been singed by Clarissa's fire—the Sacred Feminine that burnt within her. Never had I been so challenged. I could barely breathe as I returned to my room, packed, then checked out.

However, many miles later, warm breezes from the opened window of my Toyota frittered away the incised truths of the weekend: heart-fire, soul fragrance, and disorders hindering union with this new God. I turned on the radio to distract myself. Ahead of me in St. Louis was Mother, and our phone call when I arrived home. She would be relieved to hear my voice, still perceiving me as the sickly one, incompetent, and in need of her support. She need not know of my shin pain. The closer I got to St. Louis, the more my breathing shut down. I felt trapped in her world. There would be Mass, lunch, and the St. Louis Symphony next Sunday.

Yet I cherished the gift of Clarissa and her enameled heart brooch. Deeply schooled in its mysteries of purification and transformation, articulated in many cultures, she imaged a different kind of mother, fierce, tender, fully alive to worlds within and without, so different from my mother. Indeed, as storyteller, Clarissa had remained in the fire for years, welcoming others. I knew some day I would have the courage to return there. I wanted this with my whole heart, newly fired by Clarissa's brooch and sustained by her book, *Women Who Run With the Wolves*, which I still read.

Part 5

Deeper Changes,
2001–2008

24

Red Shirt And Khakis,
June 2001

The cleansing fire communicated during Clarissa's presentations that weekend at New Harmony later produced significant changes. One afternoon on my way home from a walk, I stopped at Left Bank Books. From one of the shelves, Annie Dillard's *The Writing Life* seized my attention. It turned out to be another hot read, my first exposure to the writerly process of an established author. It spoke to me like no other book. I could tolerate only a few paragraphs at a time before having to put it down.

Later a teacher of gifted children recommended William Roorbach's *Writing Life Stories* to further refine the handwritten pages about my convent years I'd composed at Ellen's urging, years before. Curiosity about becoming a writer mounted, leafing through these exercises on the components of memoir writing, still foreign to me. However, excitement soon dogged my concentration, and I shelved the book in my study for a later time.

Elizabeth

Then I began to lose interest in my work as a chaplain. When Tenet Healthcare Corporation sold our hospice program to Pathways Community Hospice in 2000, we moved to St. Louis County. Unlike my previous patients in the inner city, still up and about, these were comatose, tethered to feeding tubes, and languishing in nursing homes. Distractions assailed me as I sat by their bedsides: humming dispensers of liquid food ballooning their bodies, disinfectant smells, Muzak droning like mosquitoes, tattered mementoes and pictures left on bedside tables by their families. Rarely did they respond to my offer of support. Tired of enslavement to my paycheck and benefits, because that's what it was, I finally retired on May 10, 2001. I was over sixty-five years old. Having caught Annie Dillard's writerly fire, I knew what I had to do.

The next morning, I sat at my writing table, overlooking Lindell Boulevard, sunlight flooding my condo, the traffic humming below. In front of me, paper and pens, and Roorbach's book. I opened it to the "Introduction," and spotted two sentences I had underlined during an earlier read: "To be taught, one must be willing to learn. One must be willing to change...because to learn is to change"—advice heard during daily meetings of Alcoholics Anonymous. My hand shook as I began writing. Higher Power must be my ally in this daunting task. On my own, this was impossible.

Later that afternoon, I spotted an orange flyer attached to the door of Left Bank Books; it advertised the Summer Writers Institute at Washington University in St. Louis. However, the dates conflicted with the family's celebration of Mother's ninety-second birthday at Tan-Tar-A at Lake of the Ozarks, Missouri. I was to be her driver. Nevertheless, I would inquire further. I pulled open the door.

Inside, the friendly smell of new books and other patrons milling from one display to another piqued my energies. I could barely talk.

"By all means, take one," a clerk said. "The deadline for submissions is next week."

Fingering the orange flyer, I also managed to ask about local writing groups.

"There sure are. Two you must know about," she added, excitement tingeing her cheeks, when she had heard how I'd spent the morning. "The St. Louis Writers Guild and The St. Louis Writers Workshop. Let me give you the contact persons. You'll be in good company."

Walking home, I was ready to burst.

"You what?" Mother asked when I called her that evening.

"This is something I've got to do," I said. "It'll jumpstart my writing. I've got to begin someplace." My words faltered, despite the passion behind them. It took everything I had to back out of this family gathering, given the uncertainty of her having a ninety-third birthday. With her heart condition, she could go at any time.

"Well, if you must," she sighed. "We'll miss you." After hanging up, I shook, laughed deeply, gripped my head in my hands.

Ellen supported this development during our next hour, her wide smile bolstering my flagging spirits. Again, I was moving into the unknown.

The first morning, hot and humid, of the Summer Writers Institute, I found our classroom in Duncker Hall on the Washington University campus. I was alone as I emptied my backpack of pens, a yellow pad, and copies of writing samples submitted by me and the other students, an entrance requirement for this two-week course. Soon I would learn their take on my sample—the opening chapters about the Kenwood noviceship. No one had ever seen my work. Self-doubt undermined the boldness of my red shirt, the crispness of my khakis pressed for this occasion, clothing bought years ago without Mother's supervision.

I checked my watch. Where was everybody? Taking a swallow from my bottled water, I studied the colorless classroom with a rectangle of tables and mismatched chairs, narrow windows near the ceiling, a chalkboard with smears from a previous class.

Unable to stand the tension, I strolled in the corridor stretching my sore knees. From around the corner, animated conversations preceded some of my peers as they entered our classroom. Others soon followed and the tables filled. I took my place and watched for the arrival of the professor—a throwback to convent recreations during talking days when the superior silenced the commotion among her nuns and redirected all comments to herself.

Then a balding professor, ashen, sleepy-eyed, sauntered into the classroom, emptied his briefcase of books, a notebook, and our essays, and sat down. Buzzing around the tables stopped. "I'm Rockwell Gray," he said, checking his watch. "I'm glad to finally meet you. These materials you submitted show considerable talent. We'll continue developing them through the workshop method." He paused, then added, "There's much to learn about creative nonfiction. Perhaps you've studied some of the anthologies I recommended for this course." Feverishly, I had underlined significant passages in *The Art of Fact* and *The Art of the Essay*, in addition to the Roorbach exercises, before the opening of the course. Despite having received a master's degree in English while in the Society of the Sacred Heart, watered down as it had been with philosophy courses and principles of elementary education, I felt unprepared for the world of literature I was about to enter.

Then Rockwell scrutinized us and said, "Let's begin with introductions, your expectations for this class. Who wants to start?" Everyone stirred, looked at each other.

Across from me sat a wiry, tall man, his blue polo shirt setting off a bronzed physique. Fingering a bound manuscript, he spoke up, "I'm Don Myers. I've got this coming-of-age memoir—about my wild years as a cook on a deep-sea fishing vessel off the Newfoundland coast. Several editors have said to shorten it—I've already cut hundreds of pages," he added. "Some of my best material." He looked around the table. "I don't know what to do next. I need help." Don's passion stirred mine.

Others followed: a recent graduate from John Burroughs High School, bound for Mount Holyoke College, adept in her reflections of turbulent years spent in an adolescent psychiatric facility; a junior from Chaminade College interested in science fiction; a silver-haired contributor of food articles to *The Jewish Light*; a doctor's wife, interested in developing her essay-writing skills. Then it was my turn.

"So you're Liz Moloney!" another woman close to my age exclaimed. "I've been dying to meet you. I've never known a nun before. I read every word of your sample and wanted more." Suddenly I felt very hot beneath my red T-shirt and swallowed more water. Questions rained upon me.

"How come you became a nun? Did anyone force you to do that?" asked Don, his eyes intense.

"Why would you ever leave your lovely home for that weird place?" shot from the end of the table.

"I can't imagine being shut up in a cloister like that, away from the world. That rule of silence would have killed me!" said the doctor's wife.

"What did it feel like when those nuns dressed you as a novice? Did you really whip yourself in the tub room like you wrote about?" asked another grey-haired woman with clear-framed glasses, yet to introduce herself.

"Are you still a nun? You don't look like one!" said the John Burroughs graduate, fingering strands of her long brunette hair.

"I also have questions, Liz," Rockwell added, removing his dark-framed glasses. "There'll be plenty of time for us to get to know you and your story, since we'll be workshopping more of it in the coming days."

Perhaps Ellen had been right all along. I did have a significant story, but I still had to grow into it.

That evening I sat at my writing table, challenged by Rockwell's assignment to compose an essay on the day's impressions. I did not have to wait long. Words rushed through me. With difficulty, I captured them. It was that "other voice" with the fiery tongue, the same one that years before had produced a nature poem while attending summer school at Kenwood. A wild, foreign, untrammeled voice—it clamored for development. I still remember that momentous day.

It was July 4, 1963, a "talking day," the long tables in the refectory decorated with American flags and vases of marigolds. At breakfast, Reverend Mother Fitzgerald had challenged us to compose a poem or essay or song on the day's theme, independence, and share it during the afternoon recreation. I took up the challenge, a welcome relief from my work on my Gerard Manley Hopkins thesis.

Hunkering over my desk, I pushed aside my veil, grabbed my pen. Pressure mounted. Outside my window, ravens caught cusps of hot winds and soared—such freedom of movement within absolute control. I lowered my eyes, wildness churning within me. Imperceptibly, petitions from the Lord's Prayer surfaced in tandem with images from the Kenwood grounds I had internalized for years. Words poured from my pen until the final "Amen!" Stunned, I looked at the poem, knowing I'd not written it. But who had? Where did it come from? Perhaps my study of Hopkins had had something to do with it.

"Sisters, we meet again! Are we having fun?" Reverend Mother quipped, surveying the sea of black and white veils squatting upon campstools within the shade of the noviceship building. "For once, let's put aside speculations about the reopening of the Second Vatican Council in September—about changes in the Church—in the Society. We've other matters to tend to this afternoon." Titters melded with her last word. Novices chuckled, rubbing from their petticoats stains picked up during the scavenger hunt. "Now what about my challenge? Any takers?" My heart jumped.

Essays, poems, prayers followed in quick succession. Then a lay sister with a toothless grin finished her ditty on freedoms within the Kingdom of God and sat down. More applause. Quickly, I raised my hand, squinting into the sunlight. "Is that you, Sister Moloney?" Reverend Mother asked. "By all means, let's hear what you've composed!" My knees shook as I shared the mysterious poem; its conclusion evoked thunderous clapping. Trembling, I mashed the poem into my pocket and sat down, but not before a young professed behind me asked for a copy.

Elizabeth

That night I marveled over that poem, sitting upon the window-sill of my improvised classroom/bedroom in the Academy, wiping my brow with a cold cloth. Something wondrous had embraced me that morning, released fiery words upon scratch paper, words over which I had no control. Hours passed until I sought my hideaway bed, shadowed by the full moon. However, in no time, nastiness consumed me, compelled me to destroy the poem, seen as a temptation to pride. Besides, I had only four weeks to complete my Hopkins thesis, and I could not stand another summer school at Kenwood.

The next morning in our classroom, Rockwell settled back in his chair and said, "I sense we've made a good beginning. That assignment I gave you has a way of focusing things. Who wants to begin?" A seasoned professor, he knew students and their writerly voices, however unformed. All eyes focused upon me. There was no hiding out here.

In uncertain tones, I began, "It's called 'The Mockingbird.' You'll soon see why." Then followed anecdotes of my voiceless-ness: shamed by one of my brother's friends when fifteen years old; scotched by the rule of silence in the Society of the Sacred Heart as a young nun; overwhelmed by the chatter unleashed by Vatican II reforms; hiding out in the language of social work and theology degrees. Too terrified to develop my own voice, I had imitated others' speech, like the mockingbird mimicking other birdcalls.

However, wherever I had lived, mockingbirds assuaged my loneliness. With one more paragraph to read, I pressed on.

"Again it was their unpredictable trills that pushed me into retirement last month. Already I've begun to shake off the professional languages that have imprisoned my thoughts. Even more remarkable, while waiting for the shuttle after class yesterday, I spotted a mockingbird foraging for seeds, her voice quiet, waiting, as I too, was waiting for the emergence of my true voice. I knew I would begin to hear it among you. My deep thanks."

Silence, then soft exclamations. Like Hans Christian Andersen's "Ugly Duckling," I had finally found my kin. I would learn to write but would need help. This Institute was a beginning. Like the *mousy colorless woman* in the dream during last year's lectures in New Harmony, Indiana, I, too, had a Jungian mentor.

The Whittemore House open mic event concluded the Summer Writers Workshop, affording everyone an opportunity to read excerpts from their work and receive their peers' affirmation. I was twenty-ninth on the schedule, my hands hot from clapping.

Then the coordinator nodded in my direction. Aflame beneath my red shirt, I arranged my pages upon the podium, adjusted the microphone, and looked at my audience, seated upon armchairs, sofas, against pillows on the hardwood floor. Suddenly I sensed the urgent voice of that young bewildered nun wearing the shirt-waist dress on loan from The Tall Shop; she wanted me to tell her story. She would not have it otherwise. I began.

"Good afternoon everyone! I will read from 'The Tall Shop,' an excerpt from my memoir. About my first haircut at Maison Blanche Department Store in New Orleans, in 1968, while still a nun." I took a deep breath, knowing I had only five minutes to read.

"A breeze tickled the hem of my shirtwaist dress, crossing Canal Street with the traffic lights. Mindful of each step lest I trip, I snaked my way through shoppers until in front of me loomed the revolving doors of Maison Blanche. I grinned, catching my reflection. Imagine me in a dress! Now that I would be showing my legs, I must find a razor and begin shaving them. However, spikes of matted hair dismayed me, the result of weekly haircuts with dull scissors, alone in my room, during the ten years I had worn the habit. However with the Vicar's permission to wear secular clothes on the Tulane campus for my social work classes, this would soon change. That meant no long black habit, no celluloid headband, no veil.

"Inside the store, the glitter, lights, color, and busyness stunned me at first, until stopping at the accessories counter for directions to the beauty salon. 'Second floor, elevator to the right!' the saleslady said, abruptly turning to a wheezing customer next to me."

I paused to catch my breath and glanced at my listeners, hungry for more. My heart pounded. I turned the page and continued reading.

"More confusion on the second floor again gave me pause. Beyond the dress department, lights framed oval mirrors of the beauty salon, filled with reflections of women wearing maroon capes, their lipsticked mouths confiding secrets to their stylists. I grinned, knowing I was in the right place. Before entering the convent, I had frequented only Marie's for haircuts, a salon my mother used to frequent.

"The receptionist eyed my shaggy head, her forehead tightening, then ducked behind bottles of shampoos and conditioners to regain her composure. Uncomfortable moments passed. I had no voice. She looked up, snapped her gum, and asked, 'A haircut, honey?' I nodded. Other patrons stared, some whispering behind ringed fingers as they paged through fashion magazines, waiting for their stylists.

"Heels clicked upon the tile floor behind me. I turned around. A young man wearing a white jacket sauntered toward me, a pair of scissors dangling from his hand. 'I'm Jonathan. Follow me to my chair,' he said in desultory tones. His mincing steps and narrow shoulders hiked upon still narrower hips alarmed me.

"Feeling the snap of the cape at the nape of my neck, I became invisible, gripped my hands upon the armrests, then surreptitiously glanced up at the mirror. Looking back at me was a startled thing in need of everything, like one of my Nancy Ann Storybook Dolls my brother Tom had destroyed in a fit of rage when I was eight years old. I shut my eyes, felt myself lowered to the sink behind me, my head massaged with fragrant shampoo, warm waters rinsing my hair.

"Raising me upright, towel-dried, Jonathan pursed his lips, then began combing through uneven lengths of hair, clamping sections to my head. I lowered my gaze, hoped for the transformation only he could effect. The snipping of split ends began, very slowly. Those who had shaved my hair when I became a novice had little regard for what they were doing, just part of the drill. Everyone did it. Besides, baldness under the starched cap lessened the oppressive heat in summer. Only much later I understood how this practice denigrated the feminine, shorn of sexual power.

"At intervals, Jonathan pumped up the chair, then lowered it. Bits of hair tumbled into the folds of my cape while in the background, wailing saxophones pumped the blues. A quarter hour passed. Then another. More curls brushed my cheeks before meandering to the floor. I sneaked another look at Jonathan, his mouth more relaxed. I ducked my head again, listening to stylists laugh with customers next to me. I had nothing to say to mine. He remained silent. Another patron with ashen jowls, her dentures swimming around in her mouth, plopped into the chair next to mine, waited for her stylist. Again I glanced into the mirror, discovered a cap of wavy brown hair encircling my face. It happened!

" 'That's the best I can do!' Jonathan said, placing the scissors on the side table, unsnapping my cape. 'The rest will just have to grow out.' Should that stylist ever read this memoir, know that I was speechless with gratitude.

" 'Looks a lot better, honey! Are you satisfied?' the receptionist asked, as I handed her the convent charge card. I nodded, overwhelmed by my reflection in the mirror. A beautiful woman looked back at me and smiled."

Then I paused, paper-clipping my pages together. I had done it, despite my mouth feeling like that dusty arroyo Clarissa had referred to in her lectures.

Everyone rose to their feet and clapped, hard. Some whistled. Stunned, I gripped the podium, recalling the Kenwood community's storm of applause for my first poem. This time, however, I felt good about what I had composed. In no way would I destroy it. My identity as a writer was launched. I had only to practice, five hours daily at my writing table, to study authors of significant memoirs, and to watch for appropriate writing classes.

Despite this new direction, warmly supported by Ellen, I still did Sundays with Mother as her shortness of breath worsened, requiring longer periods of rest.

25

Crocs,
September 9, 2003

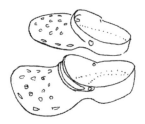

Mother continued minimizing her subtle deterioration: stains on her jackets and blouses and pants, increased forgetfulness, spoiled food in the refrigerator, missed hair appointments at Horizons, and her shuffling gait. Repeatedly, she refused my help. I stopped offering.

"I'm managing, Liz," she had said, her hooded blue eyes hardening. "I'm still able to walk over to Schnucks each morning and pick out my supper. Just takes me longer." Insults from recent falls, cuts and bruised limbs, were simply dismissed. Wan smiles wore thin beneath multiple fears. Still she would have her way. Years before, she had confided her intention to move into St. Agnes Nursing Home when no longer able to walk down the eleven flights of stairs in her building, required during fire alarms. That time had long passed.

On a dreary January Sunday, I let myself into her condo as usual to escort her to my car for Mass. A different smell assailed me. Stacked on the kitchen counter were pricey gourmet foods, bus schedules, a program from some play, and a box of pastries from Schlotsky's, known to be Mark's favorite from his old neighborhood.

"Yes," Mother said, putting on her navy beret before the hall mirror, "Mark gave up his apartment and moved in a few days ago. He insisted I needed his help. Though I still don't know." Her voice trailed away, her rouged cheeks taut. I was speechless as she put on her gloves, pulled the door shut behind us and plodded toward the elevator, breathing hard. Inside the cab she whined, "I've little space for my things. He's brought so much." I said nothing, again feeling displaced by Mark, who, on his own, had made this decision. Shortly thereafter, he changed the locks on their doors. In strong tones, he reminded me that he lived in her condo too.

Seasons passed with my chauffeuring of Mother to Sunday Mass at All Saints, Mark's parish church. Taxis were unpredictable. However reluctantly she accepted Mark's help, her attire and grooming improved. She seemed stronger, despite swimming inside of suit jackets that used to fit. Once in her usual pew, she stood straighter and smiled, looking for Mark in the choir. He was a favorite among older women parishioners.

Following pleasantries with the rotund pastor after Mass, I would drive Mother and Mark to St. Louis Bread Company for lunch, then home, because she needed her nap. There was no end of my jealousy toward Mark, who gloried in her full attention. He had become her savior, something she actually said several times when in dire straits, much later. Sunday AA meetings helped me cope, somewhat.

Then it happened, on an oppressive Sunday morning in August 2003. Mother's rouged cheeks could not mask her pallor as she adjusted the seatbelt in my air-conditioned car, then stared blankly out the window as I accelerated onto Hanley Road. To my surprise, she later accepted my arm as we walked into All Saints and settled in a pew near Mark, who was still rehearsing with the choir. Spotting Mother, he nodded and grinned, as did Christine, the director, seated at the piano, a handsome black woman with soulful eyes.

The Mass began. Mother slouched upon the pew, standing only for the gospel reading. Again she welcomed my assistance walking up for communion. But upon returning to our pew, she collapsed in my arms and lost consciousness. Involuntary tremors jerked her arms and legs; sweat formed patches of white curls on her temples. Sensing her vital organs shutting down, I coached her to move into the Light as I had done with other hospice patients. Someone brought cold cloths, a cup of water. The pastor anointed her with the sacrament of the sick. From somewhere, paramedics rushed down the aisle with a gurney, stretched Mother upon the pew, took a blood pressure reading of 64/40, started an IV. Tense moments followed. Mark watched, dumbfounded, from the choir. By this time most of the worshippers had emptied the church. At length, Mother stirred and agreed to be taken to St. Mary's emergency room. Mark rode with her in the ambulance. I followed in my car, keening.

That night, Ellen listened to my distress until there was none. At no time had I shed tears, which were still frozen in inaccessible darkness. There was more to learn, and she would be there to help me.

Elizabeth

Following an overnight stay in the cardiac unit, Mother was sent home with a change in her medications and orders to drink more water and eat more food. Grinning like a child, she was back with us. It was not her time.

With misgivings, three weeks later I slipped on my new Crocs—brown plastic clogs—zipped my suitcase, grabbed my striped wool pullover, and headed downstairs to the waiting cab. Once again, I was on my way to Boston and Gloucester and my directed retreat. Yesterday's visit with Mother in her family room was disconcerting. She wanted to tell me goodbye, despite the exhaustion harrowing her blue eyes.

That afternoon, I again settled into my simple room in the retreat wing. Outside the casement windows, the ocean feathered Brace Rock beneath an azure sky. A cawing gull reminded me I was home once again, the only home my soul had ever known since first coming here in 1984. Smiling, I sat at my desk, opened my notebook, and began writing. My morning's dream spoke of *new learning*, my consistent experience in this sacred place.

Then a soft knock on my opened door. "Liz?" I turned around. It was Richard, my Jesuit director for this retreat, tall, lean, his baldhead fringed with white hair. He was that flute-player I'd seen gamboling upon the rocks in 1984, whose soulful melodies had haunted me. Again on staff at the center, he had directed my last two retreats, marked by telling dreams and deep laughter at our foibles. "I've got a message for you. From your sister-in-law," he said, his blue eyes brimming with concern. Something was amiss. I thought of Mother. I'd waited all year for this retreat.

Richard continued in solemn tones. "Your mother's had a stroke." I gasped, gripping my pen. "It happened this morning. She's in the hospital and not in any danger. Here's your sister-in-law's cell. You can call from our office." Before leaving, he gave me a gentle hug and said he'd be available. He had abruptly lost his mother while a freshman in college.

Stunned, I later sat on a lichen-stained boulder staring at the ocean, while sprightly winds teased my short hair. The news about Mother was not good. Mark had discovered her unresponsive when he tried to waken her, then panicked and called 911. Paramedics worked on her, then transported her to St. Mary's where she was in good hands. It was unnecessary that I return home. I questioned this, knowing the unpredictable nature of strokes I'd experienced with home-care patients I'd visited for years. Repeatedly, I was told to remain in Gloucester.

Was this *the new learning* alluded to in my morning's dream? Would there be more? I slipped off my Crocs and wiggled my crooked toes in the late afternoon sun. Prayer swelled my heart. Clumps of goldenrod erupted from crevices along the rock-strewn coast. At intervals, others returning for this directed retreat waved at me, looked forward to our supper. There was no longer a happy hour, ever since the staff had woken up to alcohol abuse among the retreatants. I had been among them.

The next morning, I met Richard for direction in one of the parlors of the main house, formerly the summer mansion of the Prentiss family until it fell into disrepair and was acquired by the Jesuits of the New England Province in 1957. Atop an end table sat a vigil light flickering before Richard's icon of the Theotokos (the Mother of God) he always had with him. A compassionate smile lit his blue eyes as I settled across from him and opened my notebook.

"Liz, how're you getting along?" he asked, crossing his sandaled feet in front of him. "I'm glad you're staying on for your retreat. I sense it'll be powerful, like other years." The opened window, behind him, let out onto the great beech tree in front of the main house, its candelabra branches skirting the grass. A raven cawed.

"Yes, Richard, I'm glad too," I said, wiping sleep from my eyes, slipping off my Crocs, toeing the all-weather carpet. It had been a turbulent night. "I'm glad you're here for me. Already there's new learning."

"Another dream?"

I nodded, then opened my notebook. Already he was anticipating my dreams, shared during other retreats. Often he had said that I had my own director within, that he was not necessary.

"It goes like this," I said.

...A daughter wears a white shirt and slacks and carries her shrunken mother, crippled with rheumatoid arthritis, out of a nursing home. She seeks medical attention for her.

Richard's brow furrowed as he leaned forward in his armchair.

I continued. "The dream repulsed me, but I made myself work with it." I spoke from notes I'd written earlier, my thin voice giving me away.

"The 'daughter' is a helper, perhaps a goddess attired in white, who takes charge of a deplorable situation. She's also an inner resource powerful enough to snatch me from shaming complexes, triggered by Mother or other women in authority."

I paused, aware of Richard's soulful eyes, his slackened jaw, his folded hands. Suddenly I was very thirsty. I pressed on.

"The 'shrunken mother crippled with rheumatoid arthritis' has multiple associations. This disease, so devastating to my development, has also crippled Mother's spirit. We're both disabled crones, passive, exhausted, in need of extraordinary help."

Again I paused, fiddled with my pen, took a deep breath. I felt wasted.

I continued reading.

"And that 'nursing home' speaks of a clinical wasteland, like St. Mary's, a dumping ground for the worn out. In the dream I wanted to snatch Mother from there, to bring her into the warming Light." I paused, my voice catching, then added, "The more I learn about significant relationships around the tables of AA, the more I recognize my inability to sustain one, especially with Mother. Unlike you and your mother, I've never had a significant relationship with mine. But I yearn for this before she dies. It's been that way for a long time, as you know." My eyes smarted. I reached for the box of Kleenex. Heavy moments hung between us.

Richard's eyes encouraged me further. Taking a deep breath and waiting for footfalls in the corridor to pass, I began again.

"Then there's 'medical attention,' suggesting immersion within the Sacred Mysteries, the source of ultimate healing, rather than clinical interventions practiced in hospitals or nursing homes. That's it," I said, taking another breath and leaning back in my chair. I had no more words. A sharp breeze from the opened window suddenly teased the flame of the vigil light.

"Liz, such honesty, such courage," Richard said. "Any direction from this dream? About how you'll spend this day?"

Another long pause before I spoke. "Conceivably, the 'woman in white' will effect the needed emancipations: Mother from her ninety-four years of life, as well as my enmeshment with her. This same 'woman in white' will also be instrumental in my fully becoming woman, not the emotionally crippled one I can no longer deny."

Richard smiled, light glinting from his blue eyes. "Liz, your honesty challenges me. You might get extra rest this afternoon. Let the ocean soothe your spirit. And you know you're helping your mother more by praying for her here, rather than sitting by her bedside." I nodded, wiped a tear from my eye. "Let's keep each other in prayer," he added. "Tomorrow we'll learn more from your dreamer."

Days of sharing dreams with Richard, and ocean-sitting, passed seamlessly. Then came another call from St. Louis. It was Mark. In euphoric tones, he styled himself "our mother's principal caregiver." Then added, "Her stroke has affected her thalamus gland, leaving her speech—and taste—impaired. Her right side was also weakened. She will be transferred to rehab this afternoon for therapy and will remain there for several weeks." Then in a perfunctory manner, he said goodbye.

Immediately, I sought refuge in the woods near the ocean, then sat upon a stump and yelled to the overarching maples. Again I had been supplanted by "the favorite son." It amazed me that no one in my family thought to consult me about Mother's care, given my experience with the acutely ill and dying. It hurt, but it had always been that way. For some reason, I still needed their approval, an enmeshment there, too, which I only recognized much later. An hour passed, until at my feet I noticed yellow and white butterflies flitting around purple asters. I suddenly knew

Crocs, September 9, 2003

I could not change Mark or my family. I let go of all of them, but only for that moment. Imperceptibly, my self-pity lessened, as well as the tightness in my body. I would be available to Mark should he need me. Of more importance was my next writing course at Washington University and revising my memoir. Breathing easier, I leaned back and studied the antics of beetles near my Crocs.

The final morning of the retreat, the dawn's sky afire with lightning, jolted me from a dream. Winds whistled. Rains knifed the windows, thrashed the bushes outside. The ocean throttled the coastline. Wearily, I sat on the side of the bed, grabbed my notebook, and began writing.

Mother, still ailing, wants to have a party in her large old home. She asks me to invite my friends. I don't want to but neither do I want to displease her. Mark helps with the preparations. In a hurried manner, he pulls boxes from every closet, unwraps all her figurines, pictures, ashtrays, and places them in every room. So frenetic are Mark's movements, he overlooks plugging in the lamps. I'm distressed, but this is what Mother wants.

This *new learning* was too much. Mark's eagerness to accommodate Mother's desires irked me. For years, I had suspected he was emotionally and financially dependent upon her. The dream corroborated it. To a lesser extent, this was also true of me. That was the rub.

After returning home, I learned Mother had been unresponsive for two days, the family at her bedside. Her white-haired doctor had not expected her to survive, but she did, once again.

Elizabeth

And what a *party* would ensue for the next five years before Mother's death in 2008, a wild one fraught with intermittent crises, deepening enmeshment in the Mark-Mother dyad, and conflicts with Mark over her round-the-clock care in their home. With continuing support from Ellen, the guidance from my dreams, and the fellowship of AA, I did manage, one day at a time.

26

White Flowered Dress,
June 25, 2004

"Happy birthday to you! Happy birthday to you! Happy birthday, dear Mother! Happy birthday to you!"

Mother grinned through her fatigue at her guests seated around her dining room table, lowered her sunken blue eyes to the lemon cake with candy sprinkles that Mark had baked for her ninety-fifth birthday, blew out the candles, then grinned again. She had come far from the hot afternoon of her birth in the second-floor flat on Cabanne Avenue in North St. Louis, cooled by the Emerson fan her father bought for the occasion, an unheard-of luxury at the time. Suddenly, her eyes filmed as everyone clapped and congratulated her. She fingered the silver angel pendant around her neck, then slid her hands into the sleeves of her flowered jacket. Her cheeks flushed. Accustomed to planning her own parties, she had turned this one over to Mark, in whose care she had changed from a haggard speechless invalid to an old dowager pampered by her round-the-clock sitters, hairdresser, and masseuse.

Elizabeth

Sitting opposite her, I sucked my tongue, noting extravagant arrangements of bright flowers. "Happy birthday!" banners hung on the wall and dining-room mirror, multi-colored streamers dangled from the crystal chandelier above the table covered with party favors and confetti; and helium balloons, pink, rose, and white, tugged upon ribboned weights on the floor. Mark would not hear of our bringing dishes, seen as too pedestrian. It was to be catered, financed by Mother's charge card. For this occasion, I wore my white flowered dress with a scalloped neckline, despite Mother's disapproval of it years before, during yet another family birthday. Elated by her admirers this afternoon, she paid little heed to my dress.

"Ms. Moloney," an aproned server asked, "Do you want a slice of your mother's birthday cake?" I shook my head and took another sip of water. Weary of the prattle around me, I watched Mark grin as Mother swallowed a tiny morsel of lemon icing. Before her stroke, her appetite was only fair; afterwards, it was poor. To restore the weight she had lost, her doctor ordered daily supplements of chocolate Boost, partially frozen so she would enjoy them.

I checked my watch: mid-afternoon. Usually by this time I had completed five hours of work on my memoir and was enjoying a lunch break. It never crossed my mind, however, to absent myself from this gathering, lest I displease Mother and the family. They still shared stories of her ninety-first birthday at Tan-Tar-A that I had missed because of the Summer Writers Institute at Washington University.

A loud guffaw startled me. It was Uncle Ed, Mother's younger brother, stretching his lanky frame against the chair. In past years, this had signaled his intent to light a fat cigar. Instead, he said, "Mary, you're sure looking good!" Mother nodded wearily, her blue eyes starved for sleep. "Wait until you see what Millie and I got for your birthday! Picked it out just for you! At Saks!"

It was time for the gifts. Everyone looked strangely relieved. Mark grabbed Mother's wheeled walker, pulled her armchair back from the table, and helped her to her feet. One wobbly step at a time, she inched her way toward the living room, then plumped into an easy chair in front of gifts stacked on tables. I followed the others who encircled her with more small talk about the progress she had made with her physical therapist, who was still coming each week on a private-pay basis. Perhaps she had made progress, but her daily walks to Mass, and to Schnucks for fresh vegetables for supper, were no more.

I smoothed my full skirt around me, crossed my ankles, and took my turn smiling for Mark's camera, flash-freezing these historic moments. On everyone's mind was whether Mother would celebrate another birthday, because for six months following her stroke she had lingered at death's threshold. After much insistence, I had persuaded my other brother John, who held Mother's power of attorney, to accompany me to Kriegshauser's Funeral Home to make arrangements for her remains.

Again more titters shook the room, again from Uncle Ed and Mother's youngest sister, Aunt Jane, smartly dressed in white slacks and sweater, complimenting her short wavy hair. "Mary," she said, "I hope you liked the orchid I sent. In that vase, it should last for a while. That's what the florist said." Others joined in as Mark helped Mother unwrap her presents: gowns, a bathrobe, a St. Louis Cardinals baseball cap and miniature lunch pail filled with hard candies, new outfits to accommodate her expanding waistline, Godiva chocolates, and much more, littering the floor with ribbons and wrapping paper. Mark was in his element. Unable to take any more, I excused myself and left. No one missed me.

Later, I brought the day to an AA meeting and found relief. I always did. Rather than depend upon Ellen so much, I was learning to trust others. Afterwards, a stroll among joggers, skateboarders, and young families pushing strollers eased further tension.

That evening my phone rang. "Ms. Liz, Mrs. Moloney wants to speak with you. Here she is." It was one of her sitters. In the background, *Wheel of Fortune* blared.

"Liz, this is your mother," she said, her thready voice sucking me into her world just as if I were her chocolate Boost. "How are you, really? Don't lie to your mother. I really want to know." I saw her enthroned in her armchair in the family room, wearing her pink chenille robe and slippers, awaiting her supper, being fastidiously prepared by Mark. He'd already filled her cabinets with interesting china and colorful placemats and napkins to entice her flagging appetite, exhausted by long years of living.

I pulled the receiver from my ear, briefly dropped my head to my desk and onto the book I was studying. It was her needling again, still trying to mother the weakness she perceived in me, a past image lodged in her failing memory. In 1999, an AA friend had suggested I consult a doctor of alternative medicine. Thanks to his evaluation, I learned of the depleted condition of my body, for years aggravated by hidden allergies to wheat, dairy, and sugar. He also found heavy metal toxicity, due to silver and gold fillings in my teeth that I later had removed. With my strict diet and hydration, my supplements, my Pilates exercises each morning, I functioned better. No longer did I need medications that had never alleviated my joint pain. I had tried everything, even gold injections.

Slowly, I pulled myself up, grabbed the receiver, and said, "Hello, Mother." I heard her panting for breath.

"Where were you?" she asked, annoyance in her voice. "I thought you'd gone or we were disconnected."

"I'm here," I said in an elevated tone to accommodate her loss of hearing. "I assure you I'm very well. Perhaps you noted that during your party."

A long pause on the end of the receiver. "Oh, yeah," she said, her power imploding like a spent balloon. "Yeah."

Another pause with muffled conversations in the background. I waited, thrumming my fingers on the desk. "Ms. Liz," the sitter crooned, "Mark has just brought your mother's tray. She must eat while the food's still warm. Then take her medications. You can talk another time."

I hung up, again dropped my head to my desk, then called Ellen. Again she listened.

27

Camel Pullover,
December 2005

Again it was Sunday afternoon. Mother was seated in the family room, a lap robe tucked around shivering limbs that space heaters could not warm, her sitter adjusting the CD player on the end table. Mark was out. A wintry mix of sleet and rain pelted the windows.

"Is that new?" Mother asked of the pullover I was wearing, along with matching slacks. That question again. It irked me. Had she noticed its threadbare elbows, worn from hiking myself out of cars or chairs, she would have urged me to replace it. Unlike her, however, I was beginning to hold on to my clothes, aware that my aging body could no longer be fixed by smart clothing. That game was long over.

"No," I said, after kissing her sallow cheek and seating myself across from her. "I've worn it many times before."

"It becomes you—I haven't worn that shade in years." Exhaustion swallowed her next thought, and her snowy head drooped on her chest.

Indeed she hadn't. In June 1984, I had driven Mother to Color Me Beautiful in Westport Plaza in St. Louis County for a color analysis that had gripped the curiosity and checkbooks of women in those years. There we would learn how to enhance our complexions with appropriate cosmetics and clothing. The results shocked me: Mother's palette was spring—frothy, pastel tones; mine, autumn—rich, warm tones. As farfetched as this may sound, it was the first chink in my unconscious enmeshment with her. Her favorite colors had become mine. It never crossed my mind to experiment with others.

I looked at Mother, so different now. Her short white hair was brushed in waves from her ashen face, long bereft of cosmetics. No longer dressing, she shivered, her hands in the sleeves of her pink chenille robe, buttoned to the neck over a still heavier gown. No longer did she wear her SAS shoes; pink slippers covered her white-socked feet. No longer concerned about her figure, she had a body ballooned with chocolate Boost and special pastries Mark provided during her waking hours. Even her blue eyes were dull, heavy-lidded, as I later prayed and gave her communion. Severe shortness of breath restricted her speech. Nodding, she listened to my stories about her grandchildren.

However, the evolving story of my memoir had remained closed to her after she reviewed the opening chapters of its second draft, narrating my seventeen years in the Society of the Sacred Heart, the facts corroborated by its archives. This was in 2002. In it, she was portrayed as the caring mother; I, the daughter following a strange vocation. Never had she asked what happened behind the cloister doors at Kenwood or Villa Duchesne or the motherhouse.

Elizabeth

Mother's eyelids began fluttering, her veined hands listless in her lap. She needed her bed. A faint smile creased her thin lips as she looked at me. Unsnapping her bib, splotched by barley-vegetable soup, I helped Mother to her wheeled walker. Together we started down the hall toward her bedroom, but not without circling the dining room table first, her accustomed practice after her stroke. She always refused the wheelchair.

While following her heavy steps, her lungs heaving, I called to the sitter to turn down her bed. More wobbly steps until, enormously relieved, Mother plopped onto her bed and reached for me, her eyes glistening. We hugged. For some time, I had been telling her how beautiful she was becoming, as she surrendered her life into God's care. That afternoon, she saw me deeply, as on that night at the Seven Gables Inn; I saw her as well. We hugged again.

Then the sound of Mark's key opening the back door gave me pause. I checked my watch. It was 4:30. Rarely did he and Mother notice me when I was around.

All abustle, Mark entered Mother's bedroom, carrying bags filled with books, flyers he'd picked up during his afternoon in the Delmar Loop, and more pastries from Schlotsky's. Mother's fatigue dissipated as he took both her hands in his and bussed her cheeks. In reed-like tones, he shared the story of the movie he'd just seen at the Tivoli. Then he waddled to his room, filled with expensive art works acquired during his travels, to take a nap. Again I had become invisible.

While driving home in the ice-slick world pierced by Christmas lights, my eyes still burned. Again usurped by Mark. Yet I had had my moment with Mother. I hungered for more. Perhaps offering her living amends, after she had spurned my formal amends years before, had made a difference after all.

I still remembered that Sunday evening in her family room, following the roast beef supper Mother had prepared for my birthday. After cleaning up the kitchen, we sat on the sofa, bathed by soft lights from Stiffel lamps on the end tables, her crossword dictionary, playing cards, and devotional books on the coffee table in front of us. Beethoven's *Ninth Symphony* played from her turntable. This was the moment to share my Ninth Step amends with Mother.

"That was a delicious meal," I began. "Can you believe you're the mother of a fifty-nine-year-old? A lot of years we've shared."

She nodded, a dreamy look in her blue eyes, then crossed her knees. Her new plaid pantsuit looked especially smart, accessorized as it was with silver beads and earrings.

"And it's those years I want to speak of this evening." Around the tables of AA, I'd listened to others speak of their Ninth Step amends with significant others, how buoyant they'd felt afterwards. I hoped for the same. "You may have noticed I've not had a glass of wine for a while. That's because I'm an alcoholic. Three years ago, I joined Alcoholics Anonymous."

"What? That can't be," Mother said, firing a troubled look at me. "You're nothing like Andy. Everyone knew he had a drinking problem. His landlady finding him dead on the floor of his trailer home." I did remember my cousin Andy, who'd had warm brown eyes. Harvard-trained in business, husband, and father of four, he had lost everything to this disease of alcoholism in 1968.

Suddenly I was very uncomfortable. "It's true my alcoholism, for that's what it is, does not resemble Andy's. But I could not *not* take that second drink of wine. It always put me in the flowers, totally out of touch with the world, both within and without. Totally miserable." Mother leaned back against the sofa, silenced, perplexed. "But I'm finding a new way to live with the help of the

12 Steps of AA. One of them requires making amends to those we've hurt. And I know I've hurt you." For a moment, Mother's blue eyes misted, then hardened. "So, Mother, I want to make amends to you." She nodded, still dumbfounded.

"We've always had difficulty sharing," I began. "I own my part in it. Too preoccupied with my concerns. I want to be more available to you."

Still those hard eyes tracked each of my words like bloodhounds. My discomfort was huge. Rather than flee, I knew I had to finish. It was about "cleaning my side of the street," a phrase often heard around the tables of AA. It was about learning to live with others.

"Mother," I continued, "I've also taken you for granted. The many times you took care of me when I could not care for myself. My childhood illnesses, my broken arm, and in later years, my recoveries from knee surgeries—my broken wrist. And the outfits you bought for me, especially when I had permission to wear secular clothes in the Society. And after I left, you continued buying me clothes, fixing up my apartment, and later my condos. And all those trips to Europe, to Canada, the innumerable plays, the symphony, movies—I just took and took. You never asked for reimbursement, nor did it cross my mind to repay you. I want to be more responsible. I ask your forgiveness, Mother, for my sloth and greed."

I waited for her response, pierced by the lyrics of Schiller's "Ode to Joy," the final movement of Beethoven's *Ninth*. I had made my amends to Mother, as my first attempt.

"Liz, I, too, always wanted a closer relationship, but you kept me out. I never knew why," Mother said, her voice quivering with truth. She had found her mark. I squirmed like a trapped rat. Suddenly sirens from the street below distracted us. This was not going as I had hoped. Mother drew a deep breath, then added in firm tones, "I'm your mother. I wanted you to have nice things, and I've always had money to cover them. There's no need to repay me. Your gratitude is payment enough," she said, crossing her knees and jiggling her foot.

It was over. I think we hugged, but I'm not sure. I had hoped for more. Then *60 Minutes*, Mother's favorite TV program, filled the vacuum until I left for home. Again, we'd retreated to the safety of our self-imposed barricades.

In retrospect, however, my Ninth Step amends with Mother were not entirely fruitless. Thereafter, she nursed only one scotch-on-the-rocks during family gatherings, and later stopped drinking altogether. Untouched was Dad's liquor cabinet in the dining room.

That night I telephoned Mother, hoping for another moment like the one we shared earlier in her bedroom. Having just finished supper, the televised news in the background, she sounded different, her voice strident with control. Nevertheless I bared my heart; her response, "Such foolish talk! I'll live for a long time!" I countered with, "It's not foolishness, Mother. It's the truth." Then she said goodbye and hung up, just as her own mother had done whenever she expressed strong feeling. As a small child, I had overheard those conversations while sitting at the top of the steps in our house.

Stunned, I bundled up and walked beneath yellowing street lamps on Lindell Boulevard until exhausted. Then I returned to home and bed.

About midnight, a dream awoke me.

Elizabeth

Mother is gravely ill, and her doctor admits her to the hospital. After a short stay, she dies. Crowds attend her wake in the double parlor at Kriegshauser's, its walls lined with pink floral arrangements, sympathy cards, and donations to her favorite charities. AA friends protect me from the cocktail chatter swirling to the fourteen-foot ceilings. I know I'll be all right.

Crazed with grief, I sat up in bed. My dreamer had again confirmed the precariousness of Mother's health and her eventual death, over which I had no control. But I had support from Ellen and my AA friends from all walks of life. I had only to ask. And I did, many times. And three years later they did show up on the afternoon of her wake at Kriegshauser's.

28

Faded Jeans,
April 2006

With the burgeoning of spring, with Mark's solicitude and that of the round-the-clock sitters, Mother again dressed for short outings in her wheelchair. Next to her condo was a swimming pool landscaped with greening trees and pastel flowering plants in terracotta pots. Here the warming sun enlivened her ninety-seven-year-old bones, and she was glad, but only for short intervals. Soon exhausted by this profusion of beauty, she asked to be wheeled indoors and put to bed.

At the same time, dreams of her diminishment continued to trouble me. In them, she insisted I drive her home; in others were testy scenes at airports where she demanded bag handlers check through all her luggage to her new destination. In this one, she perished.

I'm traveling with Mother in a foreign city. It is dusk. We come across a large amphitheater and get out of the car. Busloads of tourists watch workmen assemble rigging and lights for a rock concert. In the mayhem, Mother gets separated from me. Suddenly, to the left of us, swirling waters mount, menacing in their violence. Mother grabs onto a platform and yells for help. I splash towards her, reach out for her, but the waters hurl us farther apart, then engulf her. I know I cannot rescue her without losing my life.

Other stresses also sapped my energies. Ongoing construction noises in the Lindell Terrace Condominium interfered with my writing and prompted me to put my condo on the market. Within days, it was sold. I would have to move somewhere.

A friend alerted me to a two-bedroom bungalow for lease in a quiet suburb of St. Louis. Despite its drab interior, its outdated infrastructure, I knew this would be my next home. No matter that I'd never taken care of a house or yard. I would learn. Before signing the lease, however, I put on faded jeans, gathered mops and cleaning supplies, and drove to my new house, vacant for four months. From room to room I worked, dusting blinds, washing the woodwork, and filling a trash bag with soot and spiders. My joy mounted. This place would work. I could establish a new home and finish my memoir. Mother warily followed my new plan.

The pressure was on—only three weeks to pack up the contents of my condo and spruce up my new home. Cues from within kept coming, fast. Two Men and a Truck would move my furniture and boxes. A painter I'd used in the past sent a crew to cover the taupe and raspberry walls with sunshine yellow. With help from my interior decorator, I picked out wallpaper, soft-patterned yellows, for the kitchen and bathroom. Then followed a coat of wax on the hardwood floors, original to the house, built in 1946 as a starter home for World War II veterans. Because the yard was still a mess, Nancy, my gardener friend from AA, helped me rake and bag twenty bags of leaves from the sycamore, elm, and maple trees in the front and back yards. Already tulips in the front beds were sprouting, reds and yellows, the myrtle bordering the front walk, greening.

When all was ready, my AA sponsee loaded his van with my plants, lamps, pictures, kitchenware, linens, and so much more, then helped me fill closets and drawers I'd already cleaned.

After waving him off, I heard a warm, "Hi! I'm Brandon. I live next door!" A young man in a dark business suit, his tie loosened at the neck, approached me. "I'm so glad to finally meet you," he added, smiling, offering me his large hand. "Everyone up and down the Court feels the same. We're glad you're fixing up this house."

"I'm Liz Moloney," I said, wiping my hands on my jeans. "You're the first neighbor I've met. I'm thrilled to be moving in here. It's so quiet. It'll help my writing."

"You're a writer?" Brandon asked, his hazel eyes brightening. Then I shared my reasons for leaving the Central West End, even admitting this venture was a first for me.

"Is that so!" he said. "Should you need anything, anything at all, let me or Cari, my wife, know. I used to manage a hardware store during college. I know all about caring for a house and yard." Again he offered me his great hand, grinned, and hurried up the brick walk to his home.

The Sunday afternoon before my move, still in my jeans, which had been newly washed, I visited with Mother in her family room as usual, carrying scarlet roses, her favorites, and lunch from the St. Louis Bread Company. Seated in her armchair, wearing a pearl-grey sweat suit that complemented her white wavy hair, her pasty cheeks freshened with Pond's Cold Cream, she looked askance at my low-slung jeans. She'd not seen them, a recent purchase from J. Jill's that enhanced my narrow hips and long legs. She knew better than to comment. I could feel her swallow her words and assume a pleasant smile.

"How beautiful!" she murmured smelling the roses, fatigue dulling her eyes. "You shouldn't have, Liz. I tell you that every Sunday, but you keep bringing them. You're so good to me."

Later, over cream of broccoli soup, the televised St. Louis Cardinals game in the background, she asked, "Liz, what if all this is too much for you? No support from the condo's staff. You've always had that, just as I have." I felt the needle, but squirmed to avoid its full sting. Unlike Mother's penchant for formal living, I had already created my own space in accord with the emerging Elizabeth, and I would live in it, no matter what.

Mother was not finished. "Who'll watch over you?" she asked. "I can't do it anymore. Besides, you've never cared for a house and yard before. You're seventy years old. Most people your age are moving into condos, not leaving them." I nodded, then changed the subject, as David Eckstein, her favorite Cardinals player, scored a run amidst thunderous applause in Busch Stadium. But her truth cut me off at the knees.

The following afternoon, I sat in my new study encircled by boxes of books. Cross-breezes fanned my face through the windows that opened onto the fenced-in back yard and greening grass. The move had been simple. Aware of Mark's exceptional talent for design, I had asked his help. With unexpected cheer, he had measured my furniture and the floor plan of my new house, and then drew a sketch for the movers, utilizing feng shui principles. Thus vibrant energies pulsed through my new home. Even my houseplants sunning on the glassed-in porch breathed anew. Later Mark gave me a custom-made mirror for the front hall, leading me to believe our animosity was over.

My phone rang.

"This is your mother, Liz," the breathless voice said. "I pray you won't get sick again, now that you've moved. How are your knees? Your back? You can tell your mother. You don't have to lie!"

Many times we'd been through this. Again I assured her of my well-being, invited her to visit when she was up to it, then hung up. Sparrows chirped in the junipers outside my opened windows. I was really home for the first time in my life.

During the following months, Mark seemed to accept my thanks for his help as well as his housewarming gift, but never accepted my invitations to supper. Nor did he offer to bring Mother for a visit. I did not press the issue. His aloofness returned.

The following September, my sister Martha, in town from her Toledo, Ohio, home, suggested bringing Mother for lunch. I agreed, despite my ambivalence. Her scrutiny could still undermine my fledgling efforts to stand apart from her tastes, so recently discarded.

Martha's van pulled into my driveway and stopped. They were here. With my heart in my throat, I waved to them, then opened Mother's door and unfastened her seat belt. Despite her blousy T-shirt and white slacks, her played-out smile and yellowing teeth unnerved me. Other than her engagement and wedding rings, she no longer wore jewelry, not even Mark's.

"Hi, Mother! Welcome to my home. I'm glad you were up to coming," I managed to say. Martha, quickly at my side, hugged me. Her bobbed, greying red hair gave her a boyish appearance, despite her bloated abdomen, the result of years of cola drinking.

"Great to see you again, Liz," Martha said. Living and working as a therapist in Toledo, Ohio, had precluded frequent visits until she began covering for Mark's breaks, four long weekends each year. This time he was in Nova Scotia. "Grab the wheelchair from the back seat and open it inside your house," she added. "Mother will need it when she gets there."

Then we helped Mother, breathless and weak, onto her wheeled walker, passing flowerbeds of red and white geraniums, up the front step, then settled her in her wheelchair.

"How about a look around?" Martha asked, releasing the brake on mother's wheelchair. She, too, was curious.

Mother nodded, her blue eyes filming with tears as she reached for my hand. Slowly we toured each room. "Nice touches, everywhere," she said in a whisper. "You've a real home here—so bright—so open. Is that new?" she asked, pointing toward an oil painting over the fireplace. "It wasn't in your other place." The autumnal scene pleased her, its warm tones wrought by a local artist on his way to Hermann, Missouri. She also marveled over the trails of ivy I had stenciled over the arches demarcating the rooms, the greening houseplants, moss-colored grosgrain ribbon framing the millwork around the windows, my custom-made bedspread with woven circles of greens, golds, yellows, and oranges, the highly polished hardwood floors. Despite Mother's positive response, however, I was still on edge. Her elegant gifts for my previous homes were nowhere in sight. Still boxed in the front hall closet were the Mikasa bone china and crystal water and wine goblets; tablecloths and napkins were stashed in another closet.

Then we moved into my small dining room, its French doors opening onto the glassed-in porch. Martha braked the wheelchair in front of my oval table, unfolded a napkin, and placed it upon her lap. Lunch would be a hurried affair. While heating the soup in the kitchen, I recalled memories of family gatherings at my home, honoring Mother's birthday. Then, I had brought out her gifts of linens, china, and crystal, served a gourmet meal complemented by red and white wines and Dewar's scotch. I was always relieved when everyone left, and even more so to store away the elegant stuff for next year's birthday. This afternoon, though, was the first time Mother had ever sat around a table reflecting my tastes.

After serving soup and vegetable salad and rolls, I joined Mother and Martha. Animated stories of Martha's four daughters and their families filled the room. I listened, noting Mother's trembling hand as she spooned the soup to her blue lips. Martha had forgotten her bib.

"Is this new?" Mother asked, breathlessly, pointing to the china plate in front of her, her bowed spine listing toward the table. She needed her bed, and soon. I wondered how Martha would get her home.

"No," I said, remembering the chilly afternoon my former husband and I had bought this china at the gift shop at the Missouri Botanical Garden. "I've had it for a while. I always love using it," I added.

Taking only a few forksful of greens, Mother sat back in her wheelchair and folded her hands and stared at the centerpiece of fresh tulips. Noting her largely untouched bowl and plate, I suddenly understood Mark's anxiety about keeping her fed. She was slipping. No longer could she muster speech. There were still strawberries and butter cookies. Then Martha gave me a look. She had to get Mother home.

Collapsing the wheelchair, I carried it to Martha's van, then joined her and Mother picking their way down my front walk. Martha's cheerfulness annoyed me; it always had, even while growing up; she was always clowning. My heart empty, I kissed Mother and welcomed her back whenever she felt up to it, but wondered if that would happen. I was more than exhausted; I was dispirited as I cleaned up. Yet my new home felt like a second skin in which I would learn to live a personal life.

That evening I took my accustomed place at an AA meeting in a nearby church basement. Across from me were old-timers engaging two young women, fresh from treatment centers. The smell of brewed coffee still hung on the air. Someone had baked chocolate-chip cookies.

After the preliminaries, stories began, accompanied by smiles, laughter, hesitations, knowing glances, evidence of Higher Power working in our lives.

I, too, wanted to share. "Hi, I'm Liz! I'm an alcoholic!" I said, glad to be among so many seasoned in sobriety. Long ago, I had found my voice among them; they taught me to speak from the heart, not the head.

"Hi, Liz!" everyone exclaimed in a single voice.

"Thanks for your welcome! It came off as it did!" My listeners knew what I was talking about. Giddiness seized me while scanning the faces around the table. "Thanks to Higher Power and your support, Mother experienced my new home! My new me! My sister, too!" While filling in pertinent details, my heavy heart found respite. It was always that way when I shared.

Buoyed by another twenty-four hours within the 12 Steps, I was slowly learning how to grow up, despite the awkwardness of my senior years, in my new home in St. Louis County.

29

Timex Watch,
August 26, 2007

Following hours of work on my word processor, my phone rang. It was Mark, his little-boy-voice strident with pain. "Liz, I need your help. Our mother's not doing well. Will you please check out Sunrise Assisted Living, down the street from us? See if there's a bed. She might need placement. I'm waiting for her doctor to call back."

"What's going on?" I asked, sensing his alarm, so unlike his seamless façade. There was a pregnant pause on the other end of the receiver. I imagined Mark sitting on the elevated kitchen chair he'd bought for Mother's use before her stroke, convenient for her meals, doing crossword puzzles, reading headlines from *The St. Louis Post-Dispatch*. How it galled me to see the ongoing "improvements" he'd made over the years, expensive ones paid for with Mother's charge cards. On the counter in front of him were probably numerous Post-It notes with minute directions for her meals, medications, and scheduled visitors for each day, including the physical therapist, hairdresser, and masseuse. In my perception, this was madness. My siblings said nothing.

"Mother's not herself," Mark blurted. "The sitters can't handle her agitation, visual hallucinations, her harsh demands to attend Mass at her parish. She insists others dress her. She keeps trying to stand and doesn't realize she can't. There's no reasoning with her. We're exhausted." Having experienced these behaviors in hospice patients, I was grieved to imagine them in Mother. For once, Mark needed my help. I checked my new Timex watch, more in keeping with my simpler lifestyle. I no longer wore Mother's gold one she had passed on to me following our analysis with Color Me Beautiful. Gold was not among the colors in her spring palette.

Stunned, I grabbed my car keys, and flew to Sunrise Assisted Living. Long familiarity with such places guided my interview with the director, a trendily-dressed woman with long blonde hair and airbrushed nails. She was happy to show me a private room available on the third floor, the secure area for demented patients. Despite its elegance, the faintest odor of urine annoyed me. "After a while, you get used to it," the director said after our tour, escorting me to the elevator. She was right. After providing basic information about Mother's needs, I thanked her, then returned to the Hanley Tower to give Mark the slick folder with more information about the facility. Often he reminded me that he was still "Mother's principal caregiver." It was now four o'clock.

The Hanley Tower doorman received no answer to his phone call upstairs, to announce my arrival. That was unusual because there was always someone with Mother. Sensing the drama, the manager let me into her condo. No one was there. Following a hunch, I located Mother in the emergency room at St. Mary's.

The drama mushroomed within the muggy afternoon, the sun hazed with clouds.

Mother was unresponsive, covered by a sheet, lying on a gurney in a cubicle. Mark and the sitter standing at her head looked up as I entered.

"We had to act fast," Mark said, eyeing my distress. "Mother's doctor said he couldn't prescribe over the phone. He told us to bring her here for tests." For some reason, no ambulance had been called; instead, the sitter's car had been used for the trip to St. Mary's. Then in clinical tones, Mark reported the results of Mother's chest x-ray and urinalysis. Nothing was amiss. They were still awaiting the blood workup.

Suddenly Mother's agitation returned. Still unconscious, her eyes wide open, she waved her arms in greeting to her visitors: Monsignor Tucker, the pastor who had witnessed her marriage to Dad in the St. Louis Cathedral in 1932; Father Joseph Adams, a frequent visitor in our home; and numerous nuns, even Mother Angelica, the television evangelist. To each, Mother smiled and blew kisses. Then her deceased brother Bill appeared. More excitement. Mark restrained Mother's shoulder and cooed reassuring words in her ear. Again, I was excluded. Standing on her other side, I stroked her burning forehead with a cool cloth. The second hand on the clock facing me seemed to yawn, even stop; so, too, my Timex watch. Still another nun appeared to Mother, who in her excitement almost scooted off the end of the gurney. Strong arms repositioned her, pulled the sheet over her swollen body. As suddenly as she had come to life, she became deathlike, her eyes seamed shut, her breathing somewhat helped by nasal-prong oxygen.

Elizabeth

The waiting continued for Mother's blood-test results and the in-house doctor's recommendations for her care. I curled up on a chair, again checked my watch. It was five forty-five. Mother appeared to be dying, as in numerous dreams I'd experienced for years. Perhaps it would be today.

I hurt all over.

Then the curtain of the cubicle parted. It was the chaplain who had come to give Mother the sacrament of the sick. Taking the place Mark had vacated in order to phone the family, he placed his purple stole over his black suit, then opened his prayerbook. Her anointing, four years ago at All Saints Church, came back to me, as did the memory of her body convulsing in my arms. I shuddered then as now, as the chaplain anointed Mother's forehead with holy oil, then her eyes, ears, mouth, hands, and feet, while responding to antiphonal prayers. Then came the Lord's Prayer. Through Mother's fog came the sacred words, her chapped lips pursed forming each one. With the "Amen," the chaplain assured us of his continuing prayer, and left.

More hours passed. On the other side of the curtain melded sounds of anxious visitors, moans of patients, overhead pagings, nurses and in-house doctors covering the overflow. Time sagged. Finally the doctor told us there was nothing clinically wrong with Mother that they could treat, and she could not be admitted to the hospital. So it was back home with a new prescription for agitation and a recommendation to contact her doctor in the morning. In Mark's estimation, there was no need to place Mother in Sunrise Assisted Living, no need for an ambulance to transport her home. My car would suffice.

With a heavy heart, I helped Mother dress and with others lifted her to a wheelchair. A crooked smile on her bluish lips, her eyes wide open, she had no idea what was happening. It was nine-thirty, the night hot and muggy.

More days passed. Mother's symptoms worsened, but still Mark would not consider placement in Sunrise Assisted Living, nor more skilled nursing with hospice care. Instead he conferred with her doctor and discontinued the new medication that had kept her even more drugged. He clearly wanted her with him and her sitters, despite their inability to take blood pressure readings. Again my siblings looked on, said nothing.

The following Sunday I found Mother, asleep on her left side, covered by blankets in her faded pink bedroom, the flowered drapes drawn. It was two-thirty. Ravages of near-death masked her waxen features, her spikes of white hair, her chapped lips. Only thready breathing and wheezing dehumidifiers at the foot of her bed disturbed the silence. Seated in an armchair across from Mother, the sitter mumbled gospel verses from her Bible propped beneath the solitary lamp on the end table. Mark, exhausted, was asleep in his room. I was glad to be alone with her, a cipher of her former self. Heart to heart, I surrounded her with prayer.

Suddenly Mother stirred, blinked, saw me sitting next to her. Terror constricted her eyes, like rabbits caught in a snare. She reached for me. We hugged. Sobs convulsed her. I felt my own while assuring her of God's love. Slowly her sobs subsided and she fell back onto the pillow, her eyes sweet with release. Eagerly, she reached for my hand. Sublime moments followed until sleep stole her from me. It was four-thirty.

Then I left, assured Mother was in God's protection. If she survived the night, I would somehow return. And she did, amazingly so, and even into the following year. Time wobbled as she inched toward her last breath, which kept eluding her. The more

I was around her, however, the more I felt like she was trapped, perhaps in the oversolicitude of Mark and her sitters. My siblings looked, said nothing.

The following April, 2008, I found Mother propped against pillows, the blankets pulled to her chin, mirroring a recent dream I'd had of her body sucked into an invisible tube, her face, like a death-mask, hovering in the air. Next to her bed stood the sitter, fidgeting with a bottle of chocolate Boost and a straw. Mark was out.

"Ms. Moloney," she moaned, her wide forehead fretted with perspiration. "All day your mother's refused to eat or drink. I've tried to get her to take some of this Boost. But she won't. She's got to have her medicine. Mark has a way with her when this happens. See what you can do, Ms. Moloney," she implored.

To appease her, I tried, but Mother was unresponsive; her bluish lips cracked, emitting a foul odor, evidence of decaying organs. It looked like another stroke, a bad one this time. I set aside the Boost, then pulled a chair next to her, and continued breathing prayer with her thready respirations.

An hour passed. At intervals, the sitter again picked up the Boost and teased the straw upon Mother's lips, but to no avail. Her jaw was clenched. She was elsewhere.

Mark's key in the back door broke the standoff. In dread, the sitter hurried to report to him. Sequestered in his bedroom, they spoke in subdued tones. All along, I sensed that Mother's sitters, long separated from their agencies and being handsomely paid from her estate, were in collusion with Mark's plan, perhaps an unconscious one, to keep Mother alive as long as possible. They all benefited from her financial support, although they would never admit it.

Hearing Mark's alarm, I withdrew to a corner chair and watched. Hugely distressed, he tore to Mother's bedside, the can of Boost now in his hand. Ignoring me, he commanded the sitter to help him lift Mother to a sitting position, her head flopping on her chest. Then he lifted her chin, pressed the straw upon her lips, and begged her to drink. "Please, Mother, just for me!" he said. "Please! Please! You can do it!" The more he pleaded, the more flushed his face became, the more infantile his voice. Stunned, I could only watch, knowing it was wrong.

Then Mark looked over his shoulder and said in curt tones, "Liz, come back another time!"

"I'm out of here!" I muttered. Fearing his rage, his morbid obesity, his cunning, I was no match for him. Sounds of more pleas followed me out the kitchen door.

Slowly I began to wake up. Mother was in a trajectory toward her death. It was only a question of when, and I did not need to be there. The hours by her bedside were over.

Slowly the truth of my lifelong enmeshment with Mother and my family clamored for change. It had rendered me an emotional cripple, its disorder frozen in my joints that multiple surgeries had only somewhat alleviated. For years, Ellen had advised me to detach from these unhealthy relationships, surrender them all to God in prayer. The family, too, was having a rough time, especially Mother. Eventually, I would find my true self, but it would entail more hard work. Thus I reinvested my energies into my new "family," seated around the tables of Alcoholics Anonymous, and received their support.

30

White Flowered Dress, June 25, 2008

"You'll never guess what came in the mail," I exclaimed to Ellen over the phone two months later. "Mark's doing it again. Another birthday party for Mother. Her ninety-ninth." Ellen had listened to descriptions of previous birthday parties, each one more elaborate than the last. She understood, also having an invalid mother micromanaged by a brother who had moved in with her. Expenditures for "her" needs finally led Ellen to seek legal action against him.

"Well, you have to go. You can't miss this," Ellen said. I sat back in my desk chair, flummoxed. Rarely did she tell me what to do. Wary of my closed mind, she had let me make decisions and later I had had to seek her counsel for the messes I made.

"But there's no RSVP, unlike other years," I said, fingering the handwritten pink invitation. "There's no reason to attend. I won't be missed." Memories of other birthdays for Mother, dressed to the nines, flashed before me. I had looked for the earliest opportunity to leave. My word processor awaited me at home.

Ellen's voice bristled. "You hear me, Liz? You've got to go. You'll regret it later if you don't."

"All right," I said, twisting the cord of the receiver. "If you say so. But I don't like this."

"It's not a matter of what you like or don't like," she added. "This is something you must do. Let your family see that you're standing on your own feet. Remember that God is always with you. We'll talk about what happened afterwards. Certainly more life lessons."

And there were.

Eleven-thirty, the time for Mother's party, approached. Goaded by Ellen's counsel, I backed up new material on my word processor, then threw on my white flowered dress with the scalloped neckline, the same dress I'd worn to her ninety-fourth birthday party. The usually short drive to the Hanley Tower took forever. I was still dragging my feet.

The doorman let me upstairs. My mouth was very dry. Somehow my sandaled feet carried me to the elevator, then swooshed me to the eleventh floor. Down the long corridor was Mother's condo, its front door ajar. Inside, I spotted other guests seated around the coffee table in her living room. Its faded elegance bespoke another time—the stained celery carpet, the lacy sheers on the windows, the outdated upholstered armchairs and sofa, end tables sporting lamps and Royal Dalton figurines, Mother's collectibles. Other than for her Christmas parties, this room was rarely used.

I paused inside the opened door, took a deep breath. Unmistakable aging marked her guests: vacant stares and giggles from her sister Jane, now companioned by her married daughter; her brother Ed's guffaws sounding hollow; my brother John, haggard from a thirty-pound weight loss caused by his heart surgeries, and his wife Susie, spent from the ordeal of his six-week hospitalization in Jacksonville, Florida; my recently widowed sister-in-law. Other regular guests at this yearly gathering had died or were too ill to attend. Mark was elsewhere. Suddenly, there was a pause in the chatter. Lisle, who had befriended Mother following her own mother's death in the 1980s, spotted me.

"Hello, Liz," Lisle said, rising to her feet. Others did as well, their smiles thin. "It's been a while." Knowing she was thick with Mark, I wondered how much she knew about our impasse. Already I was feeling like the outsider. Why on earth had Ellen insisted I attend this party?

Quickly I made my rounds, then found an empty chair, and a uniformed server handed me a glass of ice water. Conversations resumed as I looked around. On the coffee table sat a few wrapped gifts alongside a pair of twisted pink candles, one of Mark's additions, and an antique sterling silver humidor. A sprinkling of floral arrangements decorated the buffet, the piano, and the dining room table; on end tables and consoles were miniature Japanese fans. No balloons, confetti, streamers anywhere. No "Happy Birthday" banner draped over the dining-room mirror as in other years. Everyone sensed this would be Mother's last birthday.

Conversation limped and lapsed while we waited for Mother's appearance. I could not imagine getting her out of bed. Two months had passed since that steamy afternoon when Mark and the sitter had pulled Mother, unresponsive, to a sitting position and coerced her to sip the Boost. My siblings had not kept me informed about her continuing deterioration, nor had I asked. There was no point, given their refusal to heed my recommendations for Mother's care. Nervously, I fingered the floral pattern in my dress.

With a lull in the conversation, I heard Mark supervising the caterers in the kitchen. He emerged through the swinging door and waddled toward the dining room table, then fussed over the placecards. He appeared heavier, his shaved head glistening with perspiration. Exhaustion stooped his beefy shoulders, thrust in his tan sports coat. He seemed to be somewhere else. Still he had not seen me.

The doorbell rang. Mark checked his watch and hurried to the door to greet Wanda Becker, a professional violinist, and her accompanist, hired to entertain us with short musical pieces dear to Mother. Wanda, a slight woman draped in brown, opened her case and began tuning her violin. Her accompanist fingered the keyboard on Mother's baby grand piano, which Mother had never played.

Then Mark brightened, stood tall. Mother was coming, her flaccid body crumpled in upon itself. A smile glimmered across her bluish lips as she raised her head to her guests, then drooped it upon her sunken chest. Mark rushed over and kissed her hand, and the sitter wheeled her into the circle around the coffee table. The party began.

The musicians played chamber music interspersed with operatic arias and romantic numbers from Scotland and Ireland. Mother sat on my left. I rested my hand on her shoulder. Although tastefully dressed in an ice-green pants suit with a white blouse, her short white hair brushed from her face, she was only a shell of her former self. No longer able to wear white socks and slippers, she wore Tet Hose that sausaged her swollen feet and legs.

On and on, soulful melodies swirled among the guests, fidgeting with the programs Mark had prepared. Still seated in the dining room, he stared out the windows and kept time with the music, perhaps savoring operas and symphonies he had shared with Mother thirty years before, during her visits to his apartments in Munich and Barcelona. Indeed, her maternal love and checkbook had afforded him the good life and still did. The plump sitter, largely ignoring me, sat cooing into Mother's ear, occasionally wiping Mother's drooling lips with Kleenex; she had become "the good daughter," intimately familiar with Mother's needs.

Finally the musicians played "Danny Boy," the last number often boisterously shouted during family parties when I was a child. Listening from the top steps in my pajamas, I had known that the singers and their cigars and cigarettes would soon go home, and the house would be quiet. I never knew such partying was abnormal; some guests did not make it to their cars and slept under bushes in our front yard.

At Mark's nod, the caterers came from the kitchen with trays of finger food they presented to Mother. Weakly, she acknowledged each one before it was placed on the dining room table in front of the appropriate placecard. Then came Mother's bib, the portable table, and the plate of delicacies Mark selected for her. Kneeling in front of her, he coaxed her to eat. When he saw me, his euphoric manner vanished, but only for a moment. Of more importance were Mother's skeletal jaws, mindlessly chewing a morsel of food.

Then Mark addressed the guests, "You can see our mother is too weak for conversation. She'd appreciate receiving your wishes for her birthday, one at a time, but only after she has swallowed her food. We don't want her to choke." The sitter looked adoringly at him, then kissed Mother's cheek. Mother seemed engulfed in dreams, the only safe place for her soul. That afternoon, I learned Mother could no longer speak.

Having put in the appearance Ellen had advised, I was itching to return to the quiet of my new home and to get out of my white flowered dress, to take a brisk walk in the sun among friendly neighbors. No party guests commented on my departure. That night, I left a message of thanks on Mark's answering machine.

The next morning I awoke with a dream of another party, Mother's annual Christmas party in her elegant home with a circle drive atop a hill. Still strung out from yesterday, I recorded it in my notebook.

It is a wintry evening, December twenty-first, Mother's Christmas party in her home thronged with guests on every floor. Waiters in tuxes pass drinks and exotic treats. The noise numbs me. I do not want to be here. Carrying my ice water, I mingle with the guests, make small talk that is largely lost in the commotion. A gong announces the buffet supper. I approach the dining room, ablaze with red candles in candelabra festooned with live holly. At the doorway stands Mother, in her eighties, wearing a child's party dress with a flounced multicolored skirt, a plastic locket around her neck, abuzz with her guests who compliment her lavish table. Dad is not around. I serve a plate for myself and look for somewhere to sit. In an officious manner, Mark tells me he's saving the place next to him for Mother. I find another table.

So this was the little girl-woman to whom I had been in bondage all my life.

Part 6

The Change, 2008

31

Yellow Straw Hat,
September 10, 2008

September approached and my annual Gloucester retreat with the Jesuit, Richard Stanley. There was no farewell visit with Mother before my departure, or comments from my siblings. They knew where I could be reached. I left with my close friend, Pat Coughlin, who had been fully apprised of the impasse with my family. She'd been my companion to Gloucester, off and on, since 1986, and had introduced me to whale watching on the *Yankee Clipper* and to fish eateries up and down the coast. With Pat, I had laughed deeply into brisk winds.

"We made it again! Can you believe it?" Pat squealed as we pulled into the circle in front of the main house. "And didn't get too lost this time." We laughed, still confused by rotaries spinning us off where we did not want to go. Already bronzed from swimming over the summer, she exuded wholeness in her yellow T-shirt and khaki slacks with a Guatemalan belt.

My excitement mounted. I was home again. I could breathe.

Elizabeth

Days of prayer, of dream-sharing with Richard, of exceptional eating at Passport's, at Duckwirth's Bistro, at Tom Shea's, passed seamlessly. Spotting twenty-one Minke whales feeding off Stellwagen Bank still thrilled me; their wildness touched my own. Occasionally, I remembered Mother and the family, but not for long. They were in God's hands, not mine.

The last afternoon of the retreat, the call came. It was September 10, 2008. I sensed what was coming as I picked up the receiver.

"Thank God! When did she die?" I exclaimed to my sister Martha, twisting the cord around my finger, glorying in the sky-ocean outside the office window. My relief was huge. I laughed deeply, my eyes almost misting. Months of waiting were over, as well as months of no communication with my family. It had worked better that way. I did not need to know the details of Mother's last days. My dreamer had provided them.

"Late this morning," she said. There was a long pause. "They just left with Mother's remains. There's something I've got to tell you, Liz—you were right all along about hospice. When I got here last week to replace Mark—this time, he's in Detroit—I saw how low Mother was and called her doctor. He ordered hospice. The nurses knew what to do, especially when she died. They helped a lot."

I was glad not to have been there.

Martha continued, her voice on edge, "I ask your forgiveness, Liz. You'd been right, all along." There was a long pause.

"Of course," I said, my feelings running high. "This worked out the way it was supposed to. Sounds like you're relieved as well."

She agreed, then added, "Instead of going home from the airport tomorrow, meet us at Kriegshauser's. We'll be making the final arrangements for Mother's wake and funeral Mass." After wishing me well, she hung up. It was indeed over, and I was finally free from my enmeshment with Martha and my siblings. I no longer needed their approval. I had learned to stand apart from them.

Notebook in hand, I hurried to my boulder by the ocean, its aqua-blue hues invigorating me. I would write Mother, so newly gone from our midst. Tell her goodbye. Sentences flowed into one another.

"Mother, your life of ninety-nine years is finally over, and you've entered fuller life, glimpses of which you may have received during dreams. All the while, purifying diminishments—boredom, restlessness, knee and hip pain, devastating weakness and exhaustion, loss of memory—seared your bones, yet you complained little.

"I appreciated your deep smiles, your gratitude for the roses I brought each Sunday. There's so much more I'd have wanted to share with you. Now the book of my life is finally open for you to read, and you know the strides I've made the past months to stand apart from you and the family, to become my own woman. I hope my prayerful support of you and Mark helped. It was offered from my heart. With Jesus, you experienced 'It's finished!' from your cross. Certainly from what I just heard from Martha, you were reduced to a mass of fluids, one organ after another slowly shutting down."

A brown-speckled gull swooped overhead, cawing. I looked up, shielded my eyes from the sun, thrilled to be so at home in this wild world. Here I was deeply Woman. More words came. I continued writing until there were none. Never had I felt so well.

In the distance I spotted my friend Pat returning from an afternoon on the rocks, her pink cowgirl cap askew over her forehead, her arms juggling a blanket and backpack. I waved.

"Hey, Liz!" she called, her wide grin heartening me. She always did have a way of being fully present to me, ever since that afternoon we had met, in 1979, at the Visiting Nurse Association. Needing a practicum supervisor for her social work degree from Washington University, she had targeted me. Thus began years of sharing.

"It's over, Pat! It's really over! Mother's gone!" I said, wiping a tear from my eyes. Pat dropped her stuff on the grass and opened her arms. We hugged, her stocky body, still toasted by the sun, warming mine. "What happened? When did you find out?" she asked. My broad smile assured her that I was deeply well, freed at last to explore what remained of my life.

The news of Mother's passing spread among the retreatants. More arms opened to me, assuring me of prayer. Richard was touched.

But there was still more.

The next morning I woke with a curious dream, a parting gift from my dreamer:

... *A solemn-eyed brunette little girl is scheduled for a corrective heart procedure at Children's Hospital. Many of our relatives gather around her to wish her well. She approaches each, receives their hugs. She seeks me out and kisses me on the cheek. Then nurses take her to her room, put on her a yellow straw hat with poppies and bachelor buttons around the crown, grosgrain streamers down the back. All patients wear similar hats and smile while finger-painting in the lounges, filled with greening atriums, music, a puppet theater.*

Yellow Straw Hats, September 10, 2008

I peek through the doorway of this brunette little girl's curtained room and see she's already in bed. She winks at me. I smile...

I resonated with that "solemn-eyed brunette little girl," a hauntingly beautiful Doppelgänger of myself, certain she had a special message for me. I was beginning life without a mother. Dressing hurriedly, my pen and notebook in hand, I tore out to my spot across from Brace Rock. I began writing.

"Good morning! Your kiss warmed me earlier this morning; it invited me to approach you. In my family, I've always been the outsider as you saw in this dream. You wanted engagement with me. If this is so, please join me. Allow me to speak with you as I sense you've much to teach me."

Other words surfaced, not my own. I continued writing.

"Good morning, Elizabeth, for this is your true name, not 'Liz.' I'm delighted you called upon me. Of course I'm here to answer your questions, to deepen your self-understanding and self-acceptance. But first, take this yellow straw hat; it's like mine. Put it on. Good. It becomes you!"

I smiled and kept writing.

"Now, where shall we begin?"

Mary Elizabeth Costigan, in the arms of her mother,
Elizabeth Keane Costigan, St. Louis, Missouri. 1910.

Elizabeth

Mother's first Holy Communion Class with Bishop J. Glennon, D.D.
at Visitation Academy, St. Louis, Missouri. May 1916.
(First child with bangs seated on the front row.)

MARY ELIZABETH COSTIGAN
Baseball '23-'24-'25-'26   Basketball '25-'26
Baseball Captain '24
Class Vice-President '25-'26
P. R. D. S.   Sodality   Class Treasurer '23
Assistant Editor of Crescent   V. A. A.

Mother's graduation photo and school activities from
Visitation Academy, St. Louis, Missouri. 1926.

*Mother's gown, as Maid, for the Veiled Prophet's Ball,
St. Louis, Missouri. November 1928.*

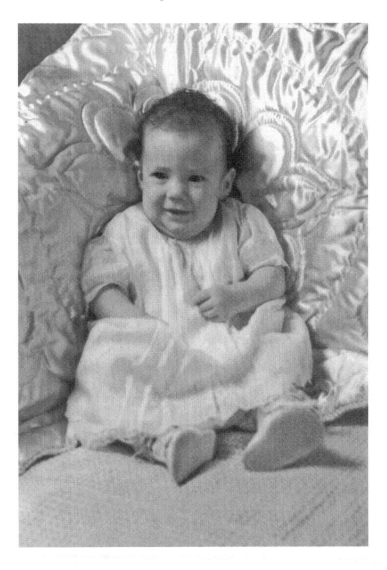

First photograph of Mary Elizabeth Moloney.
St. Louis, Missouri, 1936.

Elizabeth

Wearing yellow dotted Swiss dress in front of our home.
Brother Tom sits on step behind me. St. Louis, Missouri, 1942.

My gown, as Maid, for the Veiled Prophet's Ball, St. Louis, Missouri. November 1955.

Elizabeth

*My wedding gown for the Prise D'Habit Ceremony at the
Kenwood Noviceship, Albany, New York. March 17, 1958.*

Aspirant in the Society of the Sacred Heart,
New Orleans, Louisiana. 1964.

The Motherhouse gardens, in Rome, Italy, with my parents,
following my final profession in the Society of the Sacred Heart.
July 22, 1965.

Wearing the modified habit with Mother near the side entrance to Villa Duchesne. Easter Sunday, 1967.

*Celebrating Mother's 77th birthday at Busch Stadium.
June 25, 1985.*

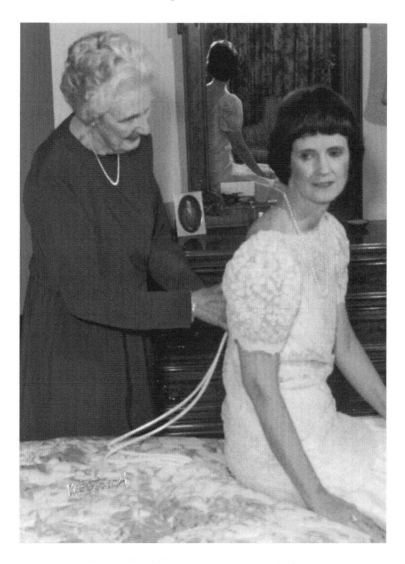

Mother dresses me before my marriage to Joe Gummersbach.
January 17, 1987.

Elizabeth

*Sunday afternoon with Mother in her family room,
1½ years after her stroke. May 2005.*

Aboard the Yankee Clipper with Pat Coughlin, whale watching in Gloucester, Massachusetts. August 2006.

Elizabeth

Free at last! Klondike State Park, Weldon Spring, Missouri. 2011.

Acknowledgments

This memoir, *Elizabeth – Learning to dress myself from the inside out*, bears the heart-prints of many:

Ellen Sheire, Jungian analyst, midwife to my story since 1988.

Professor Rockwell Gray, Washington University Summer Writers Institute.

Joan Bueckendorf, educator of gifted children, who fostered my beginnings as a writer.

Liz Craven, author, the first to critique Draft II and challenge its development into story.

St. Louis Writers Guild's monthly workshops, author presentations and memoir critique group.

St. Louis Publishers Association's monthly presentations and support.

Professor Jim Mense, Florissant Valley Community College, St. Louis, Missouri, for introducing me to creative nonfiction.

Bernadette Thibodaux, editor of Draft VI.

Carolyn Edelmann, publicist, who enlarged my sense of story and edited chapters of new material.

Helen Carter, editor of Drafts IX and X.

Anna Maria Spagna and Emily Rapp, authors and teachers with Gotham Writers Workshop, who opened me to the art of writing memoir.

Catherine Rankovic, author and teacher, who critiqued Draft XVII and later edited and copyedited Draft XVIII.

Mary Menke, owner and president of Wordabilities, LLC, for reviewing draft XVIII.

Archives of the Monastery of the Visitation, St. Louis, Missouri.

Archives of the Society of the Sacred Heart, St. Louis, Missouri.

Dr. Simon Yu and his staff with Prevention and Healing, and Mary Zorich, Pilates certified instructor, whose recommendations kept me well enough to write this memoir.

Mary McDonnell, lawyer, whose vision for my memoir kept mine alive.

Patty Rothman, Mac tutor, who taught me computer skills.

Higher Power and numerous readers of my memoir during its nine years of gestation.

Thanks to Bobbi Linkemer, book coach; Bonnie Spinola, proofreader; and Peggy Nehmen, graphic designer, for their encouragement and invaluable advice.

Notes:

For the sake of the storyline, I conflated several settings because of frequent moves within the Society of the Sacred Heart. I also combined into one character two Mistresses of Novices at Kenwood, Mothers Marie Louise Schroen and Margaret Coakley,

Acknowledgments

and later, Sister Mary David, Dominican sister, with Sister Barbara, director of the Central City project in New Orleans and former Eucharistic missionary sister. All events actually occurred.

Tradition XI in Alcoholics Anonymous reads, "Our public relations policy is based on attraction rather than promotion; we need always maintain personal anonymity at the level of press, radio, and films." Admittedly, publishing this memoir breaks my anonymity and affords readers a glimpse into my ongoing recovery from alcoholism, aided by Higher Power and the practice of the 12 Steps of Alcoholics Anonymous. Going public with this memoir was never my intent. It emerged through the consistent response of readers, also in recovery, to the early drafts, which began in 2001 and continues to this day. Nor do I seek recognition, power, or personal gain as a result of this endeavor.